THE WAY OF THE LORD

MW00677142

STEWART CUSTER

THE
WAY OF THE
LORD

journeyforth
Greenville, South Carolina

Library of Congress Cataloging-in-Publication Data

Custer, Stewart, 1931-
　The way of the Lord / Stewart Custer.
　　p. cm.
　ISBN 978-1-60682-035-3 (perfect bound pbk. : alk. paper)
　1. Christian life—Biblical teaching. 2. Bible—Devotional literature. 3. Devotional calendars. I.
Title.

　BS680.C47C87 2009
　242'.2—dc22

　　　　　　　　　2009026043

Cover Photo Credits: Nick Ng

All Scripture is quoted from the Authorized King James Version.

The Way of the Lord

Design and page layout by Nick Ng

© 2009 by BJU Press
Greenville, South Carolina 29614
JourneyForth Books is a division of BJU Press

Printed in the United States of America

ISBN 978-1-60682-035-3

15 14 13 12 11 10 9 8 7 6 5 4 3 2 1

SHEW ME THY WAYS, O LORD;
TEACH ME THY PATHS.
LEAD ME IN THY TRUTH,
AND TEACH ME:
FOR THOU ART THE GOD
OF MY SALVATION;
ON THEE
DO I WAIT ALL THE DAY.

PSALM 25:4–5

PREFACE

What does Scripture have to say about the Christian's life, the way, the path that he walks day by day? It turns out that there are a great many directions in the Bible for the believer to follow. Some paths lead home, but others do not. The following devotional thoughts from Scripture shed light on the believer's path through this world and into the next. May these thoughts draw the believer closer to God along a pathway that leads home.

JANUARY 1

Is your life a journey with a destination in mind? Or has it been aimless wandering? An old Chinese proverb says, "The journey of a thousand miles begins with a single step." That single step can be toward God. Scripture exhorts us, "O come, let us worship and bow down: let us kneel before the Lord our maker" (Ps. 95:6). That single step of submission can be the beginning of a life with purpose and direction. We need to recognize our life as a journey toward God. "Let us come before his presence with thanksgiving, and make a joyful noise unto him with psalms" (Ps. 95:2). When the disciples first met the Lord Jesus Christ, they asked Him where He dwelled. His answer was "Come and see" (John 1:39*b*). Their response to that invitation was a life of purpose and blessing. The Lord still invites, "Come unto me, all ye that labour and are heavy laden, and I will give you rest" (Matt. 11:28). "I am the way, the truth, and the life: no man cometh unto the Father, but by me" (John 14:6*b*).

PRAYER

Dear Lord, help me to walk with You throughout this year. In Jesus' name. Amen.

January 2

The Lord commanded Joshua, "This book of the law shall not depart out of thy mouth; but thou shalt meditate therein day and night, that thou mayest observe to do according to all that is written therein: for then thou shalt make thy way prosperous, and then thou shalt have good success" (Josh. 1:8). Our success on the journey of life depends on our way of thinking. If we meditate on God's Word, God can lead us to pathways of blessing. If we think merely of trinkets and things, our journey will be a wild goose chase. God led Joshua into the Promised Land; He can lead us into a land of spiritual blessing if we will meditate on His holy Word. David declared, "My mouth shall praise thee with joyful lips: when I remember thee upon my bed, and meditate on thee in the night watches" (Ps. 63:5*b*–6). We need to vow along with the psalmist, "I will meditate in thy precepts, and have respect unto thy ways" (Ps. 119:15).

Prayer

Dear Lord, help me to think of You and Your Word this day. Call to my mind the verses that I need for this day. For Jesus' sake. Amen.

January 3

The Lord Jesus Christ said, "I am the way, the truth, and the life: no man cometh unto the Father, but by me" (John 14:6*b*). Faith in Christ is the pathway to God. Man cannot find God by searching; he finds Him by believing. Jesus Christ is the revelation of His Father's love. "For God so loved the world, that he gave his only begotten Son, that whosoever believeth in him should not perish, but have everlasting life" (John 3:16). Faith in Christ accepts the gift of God, His dear Son, given for the sins of the world. For the one who accepts Christ as Savior, the rest of life is a journey toward God. The heavenly Father is waiting at the end of the pathway to receive His child into His presence by the merits of Christ, the Savior. The believer can walk his pathway in serene confidence that God is guiding his steps homeward. "Thou wilt shew me the path of life: in thy presence is fulness of joy; at thy right hand there are pleasures for evermore" (Ps. 16:11).

Prayer

Dear Lord, help me to walk with You in humble submission this day and every day. For Jesus' sake. Amen.

JANUARY 4

"**F**or the Lord knoweth the way of the righteous: but the way of the ungodly shall perish" (Ps. 1:6). The psalmist means that God knows, accepts with pleasure, the way of the righteous because it is according to His revealed will. The way of the ungodly is the way of sin and selfishness that God must condemn. Thus, the ungodly are like the chaff the wind drives away (Ps. 1:4). The righteous person delights in the law of the Lord and meditates on it day and night (Ps. 1:2). Thinking upon God's Word causes the believer to become fruitful for the Lord (v. 3). He prospers because the blessing of the Lord rests upon him. Every believer should let the Word of God guide his steps into a pathway of service and blessing. As he walks God's path for his life, he will see the hand of the Lord bless his service and testimony for Him. "He shall be like a tree planted by the rivers of waters, that bringeth forth his fruit in his season" (Ps. 1:3*a*).

PRAYER

Dear Lord, make my life like the fruitful tree that brings blessing to others. For Jesus' sake. Amen.

JANUARY 5

When Isaiah gave the prophecy of the coming kingdom of God, he said, "Many people shall go and say, Come ye, and let us go up to the mountain of the Lord . . . and he will teach us of his ways, and we will walk in his paths" (Isa. 2:3*b*, *d*). But the Lord gives an invitation to all: "Come now, and let us reason together, saith the Lord: though your sins be as scarlet, they shall be as white as snow; though they be red like crimson, they shall be as wool" (Isa. 1:18). Snow and the white wool of sheep are striking images of the cleansing power of the grace of God. All mankind stands in need of the grace and forgiveness of God. Isaiah says again, "O house of Jacob, come ye, and let us walk in the light of the Lord" (Isa. 2:5). The Lord Jesus said, "All that the Father giveth me shall come to me; and him that cometh to me I will in no wise cast out" (John 6:37). Whatever your need, come to the Lord Jesus Christ, and He will supply your need.

PRAYER

Dear Lord, grant that the blood of Jesus may cleanse my soul and make me fit to serve You. For His sake. Amen.

JANUARY 6

"**T**hou wilt shew me the path of life: in thy presence is fulness of joy; at thy right hand there are pleasures for evermore" (Ps. 16:11). Everyone walks a path through life. Some willfully choose a path of selfishness and arrogance; others choose the path of God's will for their lives. The psalmist chose to walk the path that God's Word revealed to him. He had made the Lord his portion (Ps. 16:5). Because of that he could say, "The lines are fallen unto me in pleasant places; yea, I have a goodly heritage" (Ps. 16:6). Choosing for God is always a blessed decision. The presence of the Lord is a great blessing and a protection. The psalmist could say, "I have set the Lord always before me: because he is at my right hand, I shall not be moved" (Ps. 16:8). His promise is "I will never leave thee, nor forsake thee" (Heb. 13:5*b*).

PRAYER

O Lord, help me to choose for You and to walk Your path this day. Amen.

JANUARY 7

"**B**lessed are the undefiled in the way, who walk in the law of the Lord" (Ps. 119:1). Living life in obedience to the Word of God brings immense blessing into the life of the believer. The life not only is undefiled before God, but God brings special blessing upon that believer. No wonder the psalmist prays, "Let thy tender mercies come unto me, that I may live: for thy law is my delight" (Ps. 119:77). God pours out His mercies upon the obedient believer. Walking in the way of the Lord is also a protection against sin. "They also do no iniquity: they walk in his ways" (Ps. 119:3). Solomon, in his prayer of dedication of the temple, mentioned that God showed mercy to His servants "that walk before thee with all their hearts" (2 Chron. 6:14*b*). That should still be the believer's purpose to this day.

PRAYER

O Lord, help me to live in obedience to Your holy Word this day. Amen.

JANUARY 8

"**I**n all thy ways acknowledge him, and he shall direct thy paths" (Prov. 3:6). God is able to guide the believer's path and service, but the believer must walk obediently. "Trust in the Lord with all thine heart; and lean not unto thine own understanding" (Prov. 3:5). When the believer willfully chooses for himself, he forfeits the Lord's guidance, but reverence for the will of the Lord is the right path. "A wise man will hear, and will increase learning" (Prov. 1:5*a*). The Lord can guide the path of any believer who trusts in Him. "For the Lord giveth wisdom: out of his mouth cometh knowledge and understanding" (Prov. 2:6). There is always serene peace for the believer who walks the Lord's path with faith and obedience. "He is a buckler to them that walk uprightly" (Prov. 2:7*b*). But the wicked choose the wrong path, "neither take they hold of the paths of life" (Prov. 2:19*b*).

PRAYER

O Lord, help me to choose Your path and to walk in obedience to Your will. Amen.

JANUARY 9

"**A**nd many nations shall come, and say, Come, and let us go up to the mountain of the Lord, and to the house of the God of Jacob; and he will teach us of his ways, and we will walk in his paths: for the law shall go forth of Zion, and the word of the Lord from Jerusalem" (Mic. 4:2). This is a prophecy of the worship of the nations during the future millennial reign of the Lord. During that time the nations of the world will live in submission to the will of the Lord revealed in His Word. Their path will be obedience to His Word and worship before His presence in Jerusalem. Today all believers have the privilege of worshiping the Lord in their hearts and of living their lives in obedience to His Word. Their walk should reflect their devotion to Him and their love of His Word. Paul wrote, "For to me to live is Christ, and to die is gain" (Phil. 1:21).

PRAYER

Dear Lord, help me to walk in loving obedience to Your Word this day. For Your sake. Amen.

JANUARY 10

"**A**nd when they were come up out of the water, the Spirit of the Lord caught away Philip, that the eunuch saw him no more: and he went on his way rejoicing" (Acts 8:39). His way was now the way of rejoicing in his salvation, for Philip had taken the time to explain the meaning of Scripture to him and to lead him to faith in Christ. This passage is in Scripture to show us that chance encounters may become God's way of salvation for seeking souls. All believers should keep their eyes open for opportunities to help others come to an understanding of Scripture. Others need to learn the way of salvation in the Lord Jesus Christ. The same power that transformed the Ethiopian is still at work in the Holy Scriptures. The Lord Jesus commanded, "Search the scriptures; for in them ye think ye have eternal life: and they are they which testify of me" (John 5:39).

PRAYER

Lord Jesus, help us to see You in Scripture and to trust in You for salvation. Amen.

JANUARY 11

"**T**he Lord giveth wisdom. . . . He layeth up sound wisdom for the righteous: he is a buckler to them that walk uprightly" (Prov. 2:6–7). The all-wise God is the believer's source for wisdom. Wisdom is often defined as the ability to judge soundly according to facts. God has infinite knowledge of all facts. His wisdom is supreme. The believer needs to order his life according to the wise teaching of Scripture. God's Word is a shield of protection to the obedient believer. The Lord Jesus commanded, "Search the scriptures" (John 5:39). Searching the Scriptures is the way to gain the wisdom and guidance of God. "Then shalt thou walk in thy way safely, and thy foot shall not stumble" (Prov. 3:23). The Scripture solemnly promises, "For this God is our God for ever and ever: he will be our guide even unto death" (Ps. 48:14).

PRAYER

O Lord, give Your wisdom to see our pathway and to walk humbly with You. Amen.

January 12

"**F**or none of us liveth to himself, and no man dieth to himself. For whether we live, we live unto the Lord; and whether we die, we die unto the Lord: whether we live therefore, or die, we are the Lord's" (Rom. 14:7–8). There is great assurance to the believer in the Lord Jesus Christ that his life is in the hand of God. Death does not come accidentally to any believer. The believer's purpose should be to live his life for God. The psalmist prays, "Make me to understand the way of thy precepts: so shall I talk of thy wondrous works" (Ps. 119:27). Walking in the way of the Lord is the pathway of blessing and protection for the believer. His hand guides our steps and leads us homeward. The psalmist prays a prayer fitting for us all, "Teach me, O Lord, the way of thy statutes; and I shall keep it unto the end" (Ps. 119:33).

PRAYER

O Lord, give us grace to walk Your pathway in faith and trust in Your guidance. Amen.

JANUARY 13

"**A**nd God looked upon the earth, and, behold, it was corrupt; for all flesh had corrupted his way upon the earth" (Gen. 6:12). The world is not a pretty picture before God. He looks for justice and He sees corruption. The Lord caused Jeremiah to cry out, "Thus saith the Lord of hosts, the God of Israel, Amend your ways and your doings, and I will cause you to dwell in this place" (Jer. 7:3). People must change for the better if they expect God's blessing. Solomon wrote, "Ponder the path of thy feet, and let all thy ways be established" (Prov. 4:26). If people go in a wicked way, it means divine judgment; if they will turn about and go God's way, they will find the security of God's blessing upon their way. Let us turn our hearts to God and walk His pilgrim pathway in obedience to His holy Word.

PRAYER

Turn our hearts to You, O Lord, and guide our steps in the path of Your will. Amen.

January 14

"The voice of him that crieth in the wilderness, Prepare ye the way of the Lord, make straight in the desert a highway for our God" (Isa. 40:3). This is the great messianic prophecy that will provide comfort for God's people (Isa. 40:1). "And the glory of the Lord shall be revealed, and all flesh shall see it" (Isa. 40:5*a*). That is a prophecy of the universal rule of the great Messiah in the coming kingdom. The prophet goes on to say, "He shall feed his flock like a shepherd: he shall gather the lambs with his arm, and carry them in his bosom, and shall gently lead those that are with young" (Isa. 40:11). All God's people wait for Him. "But they that wait upon the Lord shall renew their strength; they shall mount up with wings as eagles; they shall run, and not be weary; and they shall walk, and not faint" (Isa. 40:31).

Prayer

O Lord, hasten the day of Your coming and strengthen us for the walk. Amen.

JANUARY 15

"**B**lessed is the man that walketh not in the counsel of the ungodly, nor standeth in the way of sinners, nor sitteth in the seat of the scornful" (Ps. 1:1). The progression of verbs (*walk, stand, sit*) shows the progress of settling down in the way of iniquity. By stages the evil path becomes natural. But the man who delights in the law of the Lord will turn away from such a path. Instead he gains the stability of a great tree planted by the rivers of water (v. 3). He is fruitful in the service of the Lord. The Lord knows with approval the way of the righteous, but the way of the ungodly shall perish (v. 6). "The wise man's eyes are in his head; but the fool walketh in darkness" (Eccles. 2:14*a*). "For ye were sometimes darkness, but now are ye light in the Lord: walk as children of light" (Eph. 5:8).

PRAYER

O Lord, help me to avoid the darkness and to walk in Your light. Amen.

JANUARY 16

"**Y**e shall walk in all the ways which the Lord your God hath commanded you, that ye may live, and that it may be well with you, and that ye may prolong your days in the land which ye shall possess" (Deut. 5:33). These words which God commanded the Israelites to obey have their application to all God's people. Every believer needs to walk the pathway that God marks out before him. Turning aside from God's pathway always leads to disaster. Humbly walking the pathway God marks out before us always leads to His blessing. No wonder the psalmist exclaimed, "I have rejoiced in the way of thy testimonies, as much as in all riches" (Ps. 119:14). Although our way may be difficult, if it is God's appointed way, it will lead to great blessing and spiritual prosperity. God always leads His people home to Himself.

PRAYER

Guide my steps, O great Jehovah; lead me homeward to You. Amen.

JANUARY 17

"The steps of a good man are ordered by the Lord: and he delighteth in his way" (Ps. 37:23). Events in life do not happen by chance; God orders events for the benefit of His people. But they are not all happy events. "Though he fall, he shall not be utterly cast down: for the Lord upholdeth him with his hand" (Ps. 37:24). There are times when the believer learns much about the sustaining grace of God by adverse events that would crush an unsaved person. The Lord allows them so that He can demonstrate how powerful He is to deliver His people from the trials of life. "The law of his God is in his heart; none of his steps shall slide" (Ps. 37:31). God will uphold him in his faithful obedience to God's Word. He will not slip; God's path leads to blessing. God's sustaining grace will lead him home to the presence of God in glory.

PRAYER

Dear Lord, help Your people to walk the path of life trusting You for every step of the way. Amen.

JANUARY 18

"I will praise the name of God with a song. . . . The humble shall see this, and be glad: and your heart shall live that seek God" (Ps. 69:30*a*, 32). Praise to God is an appropriate seeking of God. The life believers live should manifest His praise. Even though the believer's path may be dangerous, he should pray to God for grace and help in faith as David did: "Deliver me out of the mire, and let me not sink" (Ps. 69:14*a*). David was sure that the Lord would hear him. "For the Lord heareth the poor, and despiseth not his prisoners" (Ps. 69:33). We should learn to pray as David also prayed, "Teach me thy way, O Lord; I will walk in thy truth: unite my heart to fear thy name. I will praise thee, O Lord my God" (Ps. 86:11–12).

PRAYER

O Lord, help us to walk Your way with a song in our hearts for a testimony to You. Amen.

JANUARY 19

"Lead me, O Lord, in thy righteousness because of mine enemies; make thy way straight before my face" (Ps. 5:8). This is a good prayer at all times, but especially in the morning, for this is the "morning Psalm." "My voice shalt thou hear in the morning, O Lord; in the morning will I direct my prayer unto thee, and will look up" (v. 3). Believers need to pray for God's blessing and guidance for the day. We need a straight path before us for the day's activities. The sense of God's presence and blessing may continue throughout the day. God is our King and has the right to direct our pathway. The presence of God with His people is a happy thought for believers. "But let all those that put their trust in thee rejoice: let them ever shout for joy, because thou defendest them: let them also that love thy name be joyful in thee" (Ps. 5:11).

PRAYER

O Lord, let Your presence rest upon us as a benediction throughout the day. Amen.

JANUARY 20

Jesus said, "I am the light of the world: he that followeth me shall not walk in darkness, but shall have the light of life" (John 8:12*b*). The apostle Paul reminded believers, "For ye were sometimes darkness, but now are ye light in the Lord: walk as children of light" (Eph. 5:8). The believer's life should reflect the light of the Lord in the common activities of the day. His kindness and compassion should be manifest in our daily contacts with people. Following Jesus is not a physical pathway, but a life of dedication and service. Jesus always honored His Father in His daily life. Our lives ought to be a testimony to the grace and love of God. David prayed, "Wilt not thou deliver my feet from falling, that I may walk before God in the light of the living?" (Ps. 56:13*b*). "Walk in love, as Christ also hath loved us" (Eph. 5:2*a*).

PRAYER

Lord Jesus, help us to walk in Your light on Your path of service for us. Amen.

JANUARY 21

John the Baptist came to prepare the way for the Lord Jesus Christ. "For this is he that was spoken of by the prophet Esaias, saying, The voice of one crying in the wilderness, Prepare ye the way of the Lord, make his paths straight" (Matt. 3:3). The Lord Jesus Christ is the fulfillment of all the messianic prophecies. He called people to pray to God in secret (Matt. 6:6) and to come to Himself to find rest for their souls: "Take my yoke upon you, and learn of me; for I am meek and lowly in heart: and ye shall find rest unto your souls" (Matt. 11:29). The Lord Jesus came "to minister, and to give his life a ransom for many" (Matt. 20:28*b*). This is why the apostle Paul wrote, "Therefore being justified by faith, we have peace with God through our Lord Jesus Christ" (Rom. 5:1). The way of the cross leads home.

PRAYER

Thank You, Lord, for sending Your Son Jesus to be our way of salvation. Help us to trust in Him. Amen.

January 22

Bildad warned Job against the way of the wicked: it will be cut down (Job 8:12). "So are the paths of all that forget God; and the hypocrite's hope shall perish" (Job 8:13). But Job had true faith in God; he was sure that God would deliver him. Job declared, "But he knoweth the way that I take: when he hath tried me, I shall come forth as gold" (Job 23:10). All believers must endure tests that try their faith. It is not God's purpose to destroy the faithful but to refine their faith and trust in Him. Walking by faith means that the believer may not be able to see the pathway before him, but he walks forward, trusting that God will guide his steps. God's Word provides the illumination for him to see the next step. Taking that step by faith will carry the believer to another step that will lead on to God's perfect will. We walk by faith.

PRAYER

Dear God, give us faith to walk our pathway, trusting You for every step. Amen.

JANUARY 23

"**I**n this was manifested the love of God toward us, because that God sent his only begotten Son into the world, that we might live through him" (1 John 4:9). The person who trusts in the Lord Jesus Christ as his Savior finds in Him eternal life. Only the sacrifice of the divine Son of God could atone for sin. Now it is the believer's responsibility to live his life in obedience to God's Word. John wrote to the elect lady, "I rejoiced greatly that I found of thy children walking in truth, as we have received a commandment from the Father" (2 John 4). The believer should live his life according to the teaching of God's Word. The Scriptures provide the guidance that the believer needs for his daily walk with God. We live by drawing upon the grace that comes through reading His holy Word, the Bible.

PRAYER

Dear God, give us grace to live our lives by Your Word to the glory of Jesus Christ. Amen.

JANUARY 24

The Lord said to Ezekiel, "When I say unto the wicked, Thou shalt surely die; and thou givest him not warning, nor speakest to warn the wicked from his wicked way, to save his life; the same wicked man shall die in his iniquity; but his blood will I require at thine hand" (Ezek. 3:18). Believers have a responsibility to speak out against sin and wrong doing. If their reproof is not received, they are free from that responsibility. "Yet if thou warn the wicked, and he turn not from his wickedness, nor from his wicked way, he shall die in his iniquity; but thou hast delivered thy soul" (Ezek. 3:19). God is a God of righteousness and fairness. He will not acquit the guilty, but He will bless His people who obey Him.

PRAYER

Dear God, help us to live for You and to speak out against what is wrong. Amen.

JANUARY 25

"**Y**ea, though I walk through the valley of the shadow of death, I will fear no evil: for thou art with me; thy rod and thy staff they comfort me" (Ps. 23:4). David views the believer's walk through the eyes of a sheep. The path might look dangerous, but the Shepherd was always there. He carried a rod, a short club to deal with wolves that might come near. He carried a staff with a crook at one end to rescue lambs that might fall into a crevasse. He knew the pathway perfectly; the sheep followed Him with complete trust. In the same way the believer must follow the great Shepherd of the sheep, Who is leading us homeward to the fold in the presence of His Father. The Lord Jesus Christ has never lost a sheep. His promise is "I am the good shepherd: the good shepherd giveth his life for the sheep" (John 10:11).

PRAYER

Lord Jesus, give us grace to follow You with complete trust.
Guide our steps to the Father's presence. Amen.

JANUARY 26

"**F**or therein is the righteousness of God revealed from faith to faith: as it is written, The just shall live by faith" (Rom. 1:17). No one can work his way to heaven. Guilty sinners do not merit heaven. But God has graciously provided salvation through faith in the Lord Jesus Christ. The person who trusts the Lord Jesus Christ for salvation is declared righteous by the grace of God. Christ has paid the debt of sin by His death upon the cross of Calvary. Now the believer can walk humbly with God, knowing that the Lord is leading him homeward to His presence. The apostle Paul declared, "For I am not ashamed of the gospel of Christ: for it is the power of God unto salvation to every one that believeth; to the Jew first, and also to the Greek" (Rom. 1:16). All who will trust Christ shall be saved by His death upon the cross.

PRAYER

Thank You, Lord Jesus for dying for me. Help me to trust You in everything and to follow Your pathway. Amen.

JANUARY 27

James, the brother of the Lord, wrote, "A double minded man is unstable in all his ways" (James 1:8). He understood that a believer in Christ must choose for Him and turn his back on all else. A person who is torn between two cannot make spiritual progress. That is why he commends praying with faith, "nothing wavering" (v. 6). God Himself is the perfect example of such consistency. "Every good gift and every perfect gift is from above, and cometh down from the Father of lights, with whom is no variableness, neither shadow of turning" (James 1:17). There is no trace of inconsistency in God. The believer's testimony should be just as consistent. "Let him know, that he which converteth the sinner from the error of his way shall save a soul from death, and shall hide a multitude of sins" (James 5:20).

PRAYER

Dear Lord, grant me to be consistent in my testimony for You. Give me grace to live for You alone. Amen.

JANUARY 28

David prayed, "Shew me thy ways, O Lord; teach me thy paths" (Ps. 25:4). David, as a shepherd boy and as a king, knew that he needed God's guidance. He prayed, "Lead me in thy truth, and teach me: for thou art the God of my salvation; on thee do I wait all the day" (v. 5). He was sure of God's loving care. "Good and upright is the Lord: therefore will he teach sinners in the way" (v. 8). David was sure that those who submit to God's leading would find it. "The meek will he guide in judgment: and the meek will he teach his way" (v. 9). David knew that all those who submit to God's guidance will find a blessed life. "All the paths of the Lord are mercy and truth unto such as keep his covenant and his testimonies" (v. 10). Obedience to God's Word always brings blessing.

PRAYER

O Lord, teach me to walk humbly with You on the pathway of my life. For Jesus' sake. Amen.

JANUARY 29

"**I** being in the way, the Lord led me to the house of my master's brethren" (Gen. 24:27*b*). Abraham's servant expressed his gratitude to the Lord for leading him to the very household that Abraham had sent him to find. By the leading of the Lord he had found Rebekah, who was to be Isaac's bride. He had traveled the way, not knowing the path nor the people he was supposed to find. Yet God led him to the exact person and place. This account is in Scripture to give assurance to God's people that God does lead His people in the pathway of His will for their lives. We need to live in the light of His Word and actively seek His guidance for our lives. David prayed to the Lord, "Lead me in thy truth, and teach me: for thou art the God of my salvation; on thee do I wait all the day" (Ps. 25:5).

PRAYER

Dear Lord, lead us in the pathway of Your will and help us to live in obedience to Your holy Word. Amen.

JANUARY 30

When Paul and Silas came to Philippi, they were active in winning converts for the Lord. As they went to prayer, a demon-possessed slave girl followed them and cried, "These men are the servants of the most high God, which shew unto us the way of salvation" (Acts 16:17). That was quite accurate, but Paul did not want demonic advertising and so commanded the demon to come out of her, which he did (v. 18). Her owners did not like it that she had lost her supernatural powers and raised up a riot against Paul (v. 22). He was beaten and cast into prison for preaching the gospel of salvation (v. 23). Paul went on to win the jailor to the Lord, saying, "Believe on the Lord Jesus Christ, and thou shalt be saved, and thy house" (Acts 16:31*b*). The jailor and his whole house were converted (v. 34). The proclamation of the way of salvation still brings people to the Lord Jesus Christ.

PRAYER

Lord Jesus, bless Your Word to the salvation of souls. Give us courage to speak for You. Amen.

JANUARY 31

Moses commanded the Israelites concerning the words of the law, "And thou shalt teach them diligently unto thy children, and shalt talk of them when thou sittest in thine house, and when thou walkest by the way, and when thou liest down, and when thou risest up" (Deut. 6:7). Plainly the words of Scripture should be a normal part of conversation at all times for the people of God. In reality Scripture seems to be rarely mentioned in daily conversation. But there is great comfort in Scripture in times of sorrow, great help in times of temptation, and great celebration in times of joy. Believers need to think of Scripture during the day to protect themselves from the temptations of the world, the flesh, and the Devil. "Thou wilt keep him in perfect peace, whose mind is stayed on thee: because he trusteth in thee" (Isa. 26:3).

PRAYER

O Lord, help us to think of Your holy Word and to apply it in our daily walk. For Jesus' sake. Amen.

FEBRUARY 1

John the Baptist identified himself by saying, "I am the voice of one crying in the wilderness, Make straight the way of the Lord, as said the prophet Esaias" (John 1:23). His message prepared the way for the coming of the Lord Jesus Christ. John said to his disciples concerning Jesus, "Behold the Lamb of God!" (John 1:36). One of John's disciples was Andrew, who said to his brother, Simon Peter, "We have found the Messias, which is, being interpreted, the Christ" (John 1:41). Believers today have the same precious opportunity of testifying for the Lord Jesus Christ. We are surrounded by the wilderness of unbelief; we need to be talking about the great grace of our Savior, Jesus Christ. A word fitly spoken may bring forth fruit in the lives of those who need to know about the Lord Jesus Christ.

PRAYER

O Lord, give me courage to be a voice in the present wilderness for the Lord Jesus Christ. For His sake. Amen.

February 2

The psalmist vowed, "I will sing unto the Lord as long as I live: I will sing praise to my God while I have my being" (Ps. 104:33). Too many believers praise God only on exceptional occasions. The psalmist intended to make praise to God a habit of daily life. All believers recognize that God pours out blessings day after day. Too often we just keep on receiving them without a word of thanks. All believers should make a point of praising God for grace, answers to prayer, opportunities of service. But they should also praise God for daily food, health, strength, and the friends they have. They should also thank God for times of trial and reversal, for God has promised never to forsake them. If God is always present, can we not remember to say Thank You, Lord?

Prayer

Thank You, Lord for daily blessings, for Your faithful presence with me, for the opportunity of living for You this day. Amen.

FEBRUARY 3

"What man is he that feareth the Lord? him shall he teach in the way that he shall choose" (Ps. 25:12). The man who has reverence for God will find that God teaches him the right pathway for his life. God will illuminate his pathway so that he has spiritual perception and guidance. The Scriptures themselves are a great source of guidance. The reader can often see in the lives of Bible personages the very problems he faces. Through this he can see how God can guide him through similar difficulties. "The entrance of thy words giveth light; it giveth understanding unto the simple" (Ps. 119:130). As believers read the Holy Scriptures, God can illumine their thinking so that they understand the solution for their problems. Believers need to seek the light of the Word in order to walk the pathway of God's will.

PRAYER

O Lord, let the light of Your Word shine upon my heart so that I may walk the pathway of Your will for my life. Amen.

FEBRUARY 4

"**N**ow God himself and our Father, and our Lord Jesus Christ, direct our way unto you" (1 Thess. 3:11). Paul prayed that God would direct his path to minister again to the Thessalonian believers. Modern believers rarely think of God as One Who directs their life and orders events in it. But mere chance is not the biblical way of explaining life's events. God is in control and can open doors and close them. The believer should get in the habit of praying that God lead him in the path of His will and show him the right way to go. Paul's desire for the Thessalonian believers was that God "may stablish your hearts unblameable in holiness before God, even our Father" (1 Thess. 3:13). That is a noble prayer for every believer to pray for those he desires to help. Our association with people ought to reflect our prayers for them.

PRAYER

O Lord, make us a blessing to those we live and work with.
May our lives reflect our prayers for people. Amen.

FEBRUARY 5

"The way of the just is uprightness: thou, most upright, dost weigh the path of the just. Yea, in the way of thy judgments, O Lord, have we waited for thee; the desire of our soul is to thy name, and to the remembrance of thee" (Isa. 26:7–8). The Lord is the Most Upright; His people need to live in a way that reflects His nature. We need to seek Him and to walk in the way of His will. The desire of our soul should be to honor Him. Our inward desire ought to be to reflect His loving nature and to live in a way that reminds people of Him. We need a dedicated, reverent manner of living to reflect our obedience to His will. "Thou wilt keep him in perfect peace, whose mind is stayed on thee: because he trusteth in thee. Trust ye in the Lord for ever: for in the Lord JEHOVAH is everlasting strength" (Isa. 26:3–4).

PRAYER

O Lord, help me so to live that people will know that I belong to You. Amen.

February 6

"**C**oncerning the works of men, by the word of thy lips I have kept me from the paths of the destroyer" (Ps. 17:4). Reading the Word of God protects the believer from going in the way of the Devil. The psalmist declared, "Thy word have I hid in mine heart, that I might not sin against thee" (Ps. 119:11). That is a good prayer for all believers to echo. The psalmist also prayed to the Lord, "Hold up my goings in thy paths, that my footsteps slip not" (Ps. 17:5). It is easy for any believer to slip and fall from his faithfulness. We all need to walk humbly with God and to seek His sustaining grace. The psalmist prayed also, "Shew thy marvellous lovingkindness, O thou that savest by thy right hand them which put their trust in thee from those that rise up against them" (Ps. 17:7).

Prayer

Dear God, help me to gain from Your Word the strength and wisdom that I need for today. Amen.

FEBRUARY 7

The apostle Paul wrote to the Corinthians, "For this cause have I sent unto you Timotheus, who is my beloved son, and faithful in the Lord, who shall bring you into remembrance of my ways which be in Christ, as I teach every where in every church" (1 Cor. 4:17). Paul had chosen Timothy to travel with him (Acts 16:1–3), so he would be a wellspring of information about Paul's life and preaching. He had seen that "the kingdom of God is not in word, but in power" (1 Cor. 4:20*b*). The apostle Paul is a wonderful example of faithfulness to the Lord that we can all afford to follow. Our ways need to be "in Christ" as well. We need to so live that people can tell that we belong to the Lord Jesus Christ. We need to take Paul's exhortation seriously: "Wherefore I beseech you, be ye followers of me" (1 Cor. 4:16).

PRAYER

Lord Jesus, grant that we may be faithful servants for You, following the example of Your faithful servant Paul. Amen.

FEBRUARY 8

"**H**e restoreth my soul: he leadeth me in the paths of righteousness for his name's sake" (Ps. 23:3). A believer may go in a spiritually wrong direction, but God never leads him that way. God always leads His people in the right path. He does so for his own sake; he is a God of righteousness. When a believer has gone in a wrong direction, God restores him to the right path. God always leads the believer toward Himself. The believer may think that his path is hard, but it is nowhere near as hard as the path of the wicked. Their way is dark and slippery, for the angel of the Lord is against them (Ps. 35:6). David said of the Lord, "Thy right hand hath holden me up, and thy gentleness hath made me great. Thou hast enlarged my steps under me, that my feet did not slip" (Ps. 18:35–36).

PRAYER

O Lord, guide my steps toward You and preserve my steps from slipping, for Jesus' sake. Amen.

FEBRUARY 9

"**I**f we say that we have fellowship with him, and walk in darkness, we lie, and do not the truth" (1 John 1:6). "God is light, and in him is no darkness at all" (1 John 1:5*b*). The believer must walk in the light, that is, to walk with God in humble obedience to His Word. There can be no fellowship if the believer closes his eyes to the light of God. "But if we walk in the light, as he is in the light, we have fellowship one with another, and the blood of Jesus Christ his Son cleanseth us from all sin" (1 John 1:7). To walk in the light is to walk in obedience to the Word of God. Believers can walk together in obedience to the Word of God even if they come from different backgrounds or different cultures. Obedience to the Word of God and fellowship with the redeemed is a foretaste of the heavenly realm.

PRAYER

O Lord, help us to walk in Your light and to let it shine through us to other believers. For Jesus' sake. Amen.

February 10

"Judge me, O Lord; for I have walked in mine integrity: I have trusted also in the Lord; therefore I shall not slide" (Ps. 26:1). David's confidence was in the Lord. He walked, that is, lived, his life in constant trust in the keeping power of God. He was sure that his foot would not slip because he was trusting in the Lord. He could say, "I have walked in thy truth" (Ps. 26:3*b*). His life reflected obedience to God's Word. He hated the congregation of evildoers (v. 5), but he loved the house of the Lord (v. 8). His vow was "But as for me, I will walk in mine integrity: redeem me, and be merciful unto me" (v. 11). God always responds graciously to those who walk with Him. We, too, need to walk in faith and consistency before God. Our foot will not slip if we walk with God.

PRAYER

O Lord, give me grace to walk with You in humble trust.
Keep my foot from slipping. For Jesus' sake. Amen.

FEBRUARY 11

Solomon wrote to his son, "Hear, O my son, and receive my sayings; and the years of thy life shall be many. I have taught thee in the way of wisdom; I have led thee in right paths" (Prov. 4:10–11). The guidance of a godly father can be a great blessing. "Enter not into the path of the wicked, and go not in the way of evil men" (Prov. 4:14). Every believer should avoid any path that he knows is wrong. Walking in the path of wisdom leads to the blessing of God. "Wisdom is the principal thing; therefore get wisdom: and with all thy getting get understanding" (Prov. 4:7). "The law of the Lord is perfect, converting the soul: the testimony of the Lord is sure, making wise the simple" (Ps. 19:7). Every believer needs to follow the guidance of God's Word.

PRAYER

O Lord, guide my steps; lead me in the path of Your will for my life. For Jesus' sake. Amen.

FEBRUARY 12

"**W**hy gaddest thou about so much to change thy way? thou also shalt be ashamed of Egypt, as thou wast ashamed of Assyria" (Jer. 2:36). The prophet rebuked his people for being so quick to forsake the one true God, Jehovah, for the gods of Assyria and Egypt. The Lord asks, "Can a maid forget her ornaments, or a bride her attire? yet my people have forgotten me days without number" (Jer. 2:32). These questions remind us all that we must be faithful to the one true God. There is always pressure to conform to the godless practices of human cultures, but believers today need to be faithful to the God of the Bible. The old people of God were deported to foreign lands in punishment for their idolatry. What catastrophes await the careless in the present generation? In spite of these sins, the Lord still invites His people, "Yet return again to me, saith the Lord" (Jer. 3:1).

PRAYER

O Lord, forgive our straying hearts and cause us to return to Your loving care once again. For Jesus' sake. Amen.

FEBRUARY 13

"**T**herefore thou shalt keep the commandments of the Lord thy God, to walk in his ways, and to fear him" (Deut. 8:6). Moses exhorted the Israelites to be obedient to the Word of God. In Scripture to walk is to live the life before God. Each believer is to live his life to please God, not himself. To fear God does not mean craven fear, but reverence toward God. A God-fearing person is a reverent believer. Moses added, "Beware that thou forget not the Lord thy God, in not keeping his commandments" (Deut. 8:11*a*). It is very easy for anyone to forget God and to live his life as though God does not exist. Believers should keep reminding themselves of God and of their responsibility to live for Him in the midst of this wicked world. "But thou shalt remember the Lord thy God" (Deut. 8:18*a*).

PRAYER

O Lord, give us grace to live our lives before You, to please You in all that we do. For Jesus' sake. Amen.

FEBRUARY 14

"**F**or the ways of the Lord are right, and the just shall walk in them: but the transgressors shall fall therein" (Hos. 14:9*b*). The person who walks humbly with God shall find a right pathway. People who are transgressors will stumble and fall even in a good pathway. The people who love God's Word are guided by it. David wrote concerning the righteous person, "The law of his God is in his heart; none of his steps shall slide" (Ps. 37:31). God providentially guides His people. Obedience to God's Word is a pathway that leads to greater blessing from God. But David also writes, "Mark the perfect man, and behold the upright: for the end of that man is peace" (Ps. 37:37). He also adds, "But the salvation of the righteous is of the Lord: he is their strength in the time of trouble" (Ps. 37:39).

PRAYER

O Lord, lead us in the path of Your will; help us to walk humbly with You. For Jesus' sake. Amen.

FEBRUARY 15

"**A**nd now, Israel, what doth the Lord thy God require of thee, but to fear the Lord thy God, to walk in all his ways, and to love him, and to serve the Lord thy God with all thy heart and with all thy soul" (Deut. 10:12). This question that Moses asked the Israelites touches our hearts as well. We, too, have a responsibility to reverence God, to walk in obedience to His revealed will, to love Him as He deserves, and to serve Him with all our heart and soul. God does not command extraordinary works; He asks that we walk in humble obedience to His revealed will. The holy Bible is our guidebook. As we search its pages, we can see how we can live so as to please Him. Enoch had that testimony that he pleased God (Heb. 11:5). We, too, need to please God, for He "is a rewarder of them that diligently seek him" (Heb. 11:6*b*).

PRAYER

Dear Lord Jesus, help us daily to obey Your will for us. For Your sake. Amen.

FEBRUARY 16

"**E**nter ye in at the strait gate: for wide is the gate, and broad is the way, that leadeth to destruction, and many there be which go in thereat" (Matt. 7:13). The easy path is often the selfish, dishonest one that leads to utter destruction. The great mass of people in the world are looking for the easy way out. But God summons people to Himself. His path may be hard to walk, but it leads to blessedness. "Because strait is the gate, and narrow is the way, which leadeth unto life, and few there be that find it" (Matt. 7:14). That narrow path is nothing less than God's will as revealed in Scripture. No one says that it is an easy path, but it is the only one that leads to eternal life in heaven. It is the only path in which the believer can walk with God.

PRAYER

O Lord, give us grace that we may walk with You day by day. Keep us on that straight and narrow path. For Jesus' sake. Amen.

FEBRUARY 17

"**W**herewithal shall a young man cleanse his way? by taking heed thereto according to thy word" (Ps. 119:9). Filling the mind with God's Word has a powerful cleansing effect. And it is not just young men that need such cleansing. Old men, women, and children need the cleansing power of the Holy Scriptures. The Word of God crowds out what is wrong and fills the mind instead with thoughts of God, righteousness, and heaven. The psalmist goes on to say, "Thy word have I hid in mine heart, that I might not sin against thee" (Ps. 119:11). The Word of God is powerful enough to crowd out thoughts that dishonor God. Serenity and peace come from meditating on God's Word. The Word of God causes all who ponder it to focus on God and His will. As the mind is cleansed, so the way is cleansed as well.

PRAYER

O Lord, help me to think about Your Word and to let its truth work out in my life. For Jesus' sake. Amen.

FEBRUARY 18

The book of Judges describes how the Israelites forsook the Lord and served Baal (Judg. 2:13), yet the Lord raised up judges to deliver them (v. 16). "And yet they would not hearken unto their judges, but they went a whoring after other gods, and bowed themselves unto them: they turned quickly out of the way which their fathers walked in, obeying the commandments of the Lord; but they did not so" (Judg. 2:17). The Lord raised up judges to deliver them, but as soon as the judge died, they returned to their wicked ways (v. 19). So the Lord left the wicked nations in the land, "that through them I may prove Israel, whether they will keep the way of the Lord to walk therein, as their fathers did keep it, or not" (Judg. 2:22). All believers should remember that the Lord still leaves the wicked in the land to test His people to see if they will walk in His ways or not.

PRAYER

O Lord, give us grace to walk with You in the midst of a wicked world. For Jesus' sake. Amen.

FEBRUARY 19

The apostle Paul writes concerning lost people who know not God, "Destruction and misery are in their ways: and the way of peace have they not known" (Rom. 3:16–17). The lost person is sunk in misery; he cannot find the way of peace because he does not know the Prince of peace (Isa. 9:6), the Lord Jesus Christ. He said to His disciples in the upper room, "Peace I leave with you, my peace I give unto you: not as the world giveth, give I unto you. Let not your heart be troubled, neither let it be afraid" (John 14:27). When the Lord Jesus came to the disciples after His resurrection, His first word was "Peace be unto you" (John 20:19*b*). The apostle Paul referred to Christ's sacrifice for sin, "For he is our peace" (Eph. 2:14*a*). He prayed, "Now the Lord of peace himself give you peace always" (2 Thess. 3:16*a*).

PRAYER

Dear Lord Jesus, we thank You for being our peace and for imparting that peace to us. We praise Your holy name. Amen.

FEBRUARY 20

"**I**f we live in the Spirit, let us also walk in the Spirit" (Gal. 5:25). The believer must not trust in himself but instead trust in the power and grace of God in his life. That means manifesting the fruit of the Spirit in his life. "But the fruit of the Spirit is love, joy, peace, longsuffering, gentleness, goodness, faith, meekness, temperance" (Gal. 5:22–23*a*). This is the very character of Christ that the Spirit forms within the believer. The Holy Spirit must be the motivating power in the life of every believer. Mere self-effort does not accomplish anything in the Christian's life. The Spirit of God must "grow" the character of Christ in the believer for him to have a testimony for Christ in this wicked world. It is by the Holy Spirit that the believer can be a testimony for Christ.

PRAYER

Dear Lord, let Your Holy Spirit empower my walk that I may honor You this day in all that I do. Amen.

FEBRUARY 21

The Lord Jesus said, "Agree with thine adversary quickly, whiles thou art in the way with him; lest at any time the adversary deliver thee to the judge, and the judge deliver thee to the officer, and thou be cast into prison" (Matt. 5:25). If there is a genuine complaint against a believer, he should settle the matter promptly, while in the way, and not wait to be dragged into court and forced to pay. A cheerful and caring attitude is a good testimony for the Lord Jesus Christ. The believer should be a good citizen as well as a faithful believer in Christ. Devotion to God does not contradict being a good testimony in the sight of men. Instead, honorable conduct in the sight of men reinforces the testimony of religious devotion to God.

PRAYER

O Lord, help us to be good citizens as well as devout believers in You. For Jesus' sake. Amen.

FEBRUARY 22

"The Lord executeth righteousness. . . . He made known his ways unto Moses, his acts unto the children of Israel" (Ps. 103:6–7). God is a God of righteousness. He revealed His righteous ways to Moses, but the children of Israel saw only His acts. They did not understand what the Lord was doing. Moses had the spiritual perception to understand the providential meaning of God's actions. Believers today need this spiritual perception to understand the providential actions of God. He still leads His people and guides them through the wilderness of this world. We need that spiritual perception that comes from searching the Scriptures to know the will of God. "Thy word is a lamp unto my feet, and a light unto my path" (Ps. 119:105).

PRAYER

O Lord, open my eyes to Your Word that I may understand the path You intend me to walk. For Jesus' sake. Amen.

FEBRUARY 23

David wrote, "For I have kept the ways of the Lord, and have not wickedly departed from my God" (Ps. 18:21). David loved the Lord, for he found that the Lord was his rock, his fortress, and his deliverer (v. 2). He had been through deep sorrow (vv. 4–5), but he had called upon the Lord for deliverance (v. 6). Now he could testify that God "sent from above, he took me, he drew me out of many waters. He delivered me from my strong enemy" (Ps. 18:16*b*–17*a*). God's people should remember that God is able to deliver them from all their trials. David testified, "The Lord was my stay" (Ps. 18:18*b*). Believers today need to trust in the Lord the way David did. It does not matter how dark the pathway may look. David declared, "For thou wilt light my candle: the Lord my God will enlighten my darkness" (Ps. 18:28).

PRAYER

O Lord, enlighten us in our darkness and deliver us in our trials. For Jesus' sake. Amen.

FEBRUARY 24

David vowed, "I will behave myself wisely in a perfect way. O when wilt thou come unto me? I will walk within my house with a perfect heart" (Ps. 101:2). All people should think seriously about the influence of their life upon the lives of their family. David determined to be an influence for good in his family. He declared, "I will set no wicked thing before mine eyes" (Ps. 101:3*a*). That declaration ought to influence what kinds of TV programs are allowed in the home. David directed his attention to the kind of people he would work with. "Mine eyes shall be upon the faithful of the land, that they may dwell with me: he that walketh in a perfect way, he shall serve me" (Ps. 101:6). God's people should help and strengthen one another in their stand for God.

PRAYER

O Lord, help us to live for You in our homes and workplaces. May our lives be a testimony for all who know us. For Jesus' sake. Amen.

FEBRUARY 25

"**H**e keepeth the paths of judgment, and preserveth the way of his saints" (Prov. 2:8). Solomon was writing about the Lord, Who gives wisdom and lays up wisdom for the righteous (Prov. 2:6–7). God guards and preserves the way of His people. An important way that God does this is by imparting His wisdom to His people. People who act foolishly act contrary to God's revealed wisdom. When wisdom enters the heart of the believer, discretion and understanding shall preserve him (vv. 10–11). Reverence for the Lord is the beginning of wisdom (Ps. 111:10*a*). James declares, "If any of you lack wisdom, let him ask of God, that giveth to all men liberally, and upbraideth not; and it shall be given him" (James 1:5). He adds, "But let him ask in faith, nothing wavering" (v. 6*a*).

PRAYER

O Lord, grant us Your wisdom that we may walk according to Your Word in humble obedience. For Jesus' sake. Amen.

FEBRUARY 26

"**F**or the Lord spake thus to me with a strong hand, and instructed me that I should not walk in the way of this people, saying, Say ye not, A confederacy" (Isa. 8:11–12). The people of Judah were tempted to make a confederacy with Israel, the Northern Kingdom, and with Syria against the Assyrian empire. It would do no good; the Assyrians would crush them all. Instead Isaiah urged, "Sanctify the Lord of hosts himself; and let him be your fear, and let him be your dread" (Isa. 8:13). Jehovah, the Lord of hosts, is the protection of His people. In our own day there is still a tendency to trust in human means. Political alliances, business deals, and other human devices are still the trust of many. The believer ought to trust in God to guide his steps and protect his way. "Thou art my portion, O Lord: I have said that I would keep thy words" (Ps. 119:57).

PRAYER

O Lord, protect Your people and lead us in the path of Your will. For Jesus' sake. Amen.

FEBRUARY 27

The apostle Paul said, "O full of all subtilty and all mischief, thou child of the devil, thou enemy of all righteousness, wilt thou not cease to pervert the right ways of the Lord?" (Acts 13:10). Satan worshippers and cultists still do all they can to attack and discredit the Bible. But the right ways of the Lord manifest the fruit of the Spirit: "love, joy, peace, longsuffering, gentleness, goodness, faith, meekness, temperance" (Gal. 5:22*b*–23*a*). The character of Christ may be seen in His people. That includes speaking out against what is wrong. The Lord Jesus rebuked arrogance and hypocrisy; His people should certainly stand for what is right and protest against wrong. They need to be the salt that holds back the corruption of the world.

PRAYER

O Lord, give Your people the boldness to stand for what is right and to protest against wrong wherever it is found. For Jesus' sake. Amen.

FEBRUARY 28

"When Samuel was old . . . his sons walked not in his ways, but turned aside after lucre, and took bribes, and perverted judgment" (1 Sam. 8:1b, 3b). It was a heartbreak to Samuel to see his sons turn away from the Lord and pervert justice. But he assisted the people in finding a king and helping Saul to set up his reign. Many times God calls His people to perform sad tasks. He never forsakes them and often uses them again to perform joyous tasks. It was Samuel who anointed David to be king in Saul's place (1 Sam. 16:13). It was David who said of God, "He leadeth me in the paths of righteousness for his name's sake" (Ps. 23:3b). God still leads His people in paths of righteousness. We must trust Him to lead us in His path for our lives so that His blessing may rest upon us.

PRAYER

O Lord, lead us in the path of Your will that our lives may be a blessing to all who know us. For Jesus' sake. Amen.

FEBRUARY 29

It may be disconcerting to see your birth date disappear from the calendar, but you will never disappear from the eye of God. Hagar fled from Sarah into the way of the desert, but the angel of the Lord appeared to help her (Gen. 16:7). She called him "Thou God seest me" (Gen. 16:13). David wrote, "If I take the wings of the morning, and dwell in the uttermost parts of the sea; Even there shall thy hand lead me, and thy right hand shall hold me" (Ps. 139:9–10). David also wrote, "The Lord is nigh unto all them that call upon him, to all that call upon him in truth" (Ps. 145:18). The writer to the Hebrews exhorts us, "Let us therefore come boldly unto the throne of grace, that we may obtain mercy, and find grace to help in time of need" (Heb. 4:16).

PRAYER

Thank You, Lord, for hearing my prayers and caring for me, even when others forget. Help me to walk with You through life. For Jesus' sake. Amen.

MARCH 1

"**T**he priests said not, Where is the Lord? and they that handle the law knew me not: the pastors also transgressed against me, and the prophets prophesied by Baal, and walked after things that do not profit" (Jer. 2:8). That sounds like today's situation. Religious leaders do not seek the God of the Bible. Unconverted pastors lead the flock astray. The Lord responded, "Wherefore I will yet plead with you, saith the Lord" (Jer. 2:9). It would be a pleading with judgment. The Lord asked, "Why gaddest thou about so much to change thy way? thou also shalt be ashamed of Egypt, as thou wast ashamed of Assyria" (Jer. 2:36). The people tried to get help from Assyria and failed; now they seek help from Egypt, and will fail again. God charges, "My people have forgotten me days without number" (Jer. 2:32). We should walk in the way of the Lord and seek Him alone.

PRAYER

O Lord, turn our steps in Your direction and help us to seek You with a single-minded heart. For Jesus' sake. Amen.

MARCH 2

"**T**each me thy way, O Lord, and lead me in a plain path, because of mine enemies" (Ps. 27:11). The believer needs the instruction of God's Word in order to live his life for God. There are always enemies who would like to see us fall. But God sustains His people and leads them with clear direction from His Word. The psalmist exhorts, "Wait on the Lord: be of good courage, and he shall strengthen thine heart: wait, I say, on the Lord" (Ps. 27:14). All believers need the patience of waiting on God. The psalmist also prays, "Uphold me according unto thy word, that I may live: and let me not be ashamed of my hope" (Ps. 119:116). God will keep the promise of His Word and will sustain His people. We need to walk with patience the path He sets before us.

PRAYER

Thank You, Lord, for guiding our steps by Your Word. Help us to see Your path and to walk it in patience. For Jesus' sake. Amen.

MARCH 3

The apostles explained that God "in times past suffered all nations to walk in their own ways" (Acts 14:16), but they preached the gospel of salvation to all who would listen (Acts 14:21). God is not far away, "For in him we live, and move, and have our being" (Acts 17:28). God promises, "Call upon me in the day of trouble: I will deliver thee, and thou shalt glorify me" (Ps. 50:15). Paul exhorted believers, "I beseech you therefore, brethren, by the mercies of God, that ye present your bodies a living sacrifice, holy, acceptable unto God, which is your reasonable service" (Rom. 12:1). "But put ye on the Lord Jesus Christ, and make not provision for the flesh, to fulfil the lusts thereof" (Rom. 13:14).

PRAYER

O Lord, help us to walk in Your way by the grace of the Lord Jesus Christ. Preserve us from going astray and lead us to Your home for us. Amen.

MARCH 4

"**S**o he [God] drove out the man; and he placed at the east of the garden of Eden Cherubims, and a flaming sword which turned every way, to keep the way of the tree of life" (Gen. 3:24). God is holy and cannot tolerate sin. He is also the giver of life. He will not allow man to steal life. Instead, God offers to give life to man through His Son, the Lord Jesus Christ. Jesus said, "I am the bread of life: he that cometh to me shall never hunger; and he that believeth on me shall never thirst" (John 6:35). Jesus prayed, "And this is life eternal, that they might know thee the only true God, and Jesus Christ, whom thou hast sent" (John 17:3). Paul wrote, "For the wages of sin is death; but the gift of God is eternal life through Jesus Christ our Lord" (Rom. 6:23).

PRAYER

Thank You, Lord, for providing eternal life through the sacrifice of Your Son, the Lord Jesus Christ. Help us to live in the light of that gift. Amen.

MARCH 5

The writer to the Hebrews quotes from Ps. 95:8, "Harden not your hearts, as in the provocation, in the day of temptation in the wilderness" (Heb. 3:8). He continues to quote, "They do alway err in their heart; and they have not known my ways" (Heb. 3:10*b*; Ps. 95:10). He goes on to exhort all believers, "Take heed, brethren, lest there be in any of you an evil heart of unbelief, in departing from the living God" (Heb. 3:12). The believer needs to maintain a tender heart before God and His holy Word. Every believer should walk in God's ways in obedience to His holy Word. The heart of every believer should be devoted to God. The writer to the Hebrews exhorts us, "Let us therefore come boldly unto the throne of grace, that we may obtain mercy, and find grace to help in time of need" (Heb. 4:16).

PRAYER

O Lord, give us the grace we need to live our lives in obedience to Your holy Word. Give us a tender heart of obedience to You. For Jesus' sake. Amen.

MARCH 6

The servant answered Saul, "Behold, I have here at hand the fourth part of a shekel of silver: that will I give to the man of God, to tell us our way" (1 Sam. 9:8). Saul and his servant were seeking lost asses. They decided to ask the prophet Samuel where to seek for them. It is always a good practice to seek advice from those who serve God. Samuel told them that the asses were already found (v. 20). But Samuel had a more serious message for Saul about his coming responsibility as king of Israel (1 Sam. 10:1). God knows the pathway of every person on earth. He guides the steps of His people. All should seek His guidance for the path they take in life. The psalmist prayed, "Turn away mine eyes from beholding vanity; and quicken thou me in thy way" (Ps. 119:37).

PRAYER

O Lord, help me to walk in the path of Your will for my life. Guide my steps by Your Word. For Jesus' sake. Amen.

MARCH 7

"**T**his I say then, Walk in the Spirit, and ye shall not fulfil the lust of the flesh" (Gal. 5:16). Living the life under the control of the Spirit of God means that the believer will not be sunk in the sins of the flesh. There is a constant battle between the flesh and the spirit in the life of every believer (Gal. 5:17). When the believer allows the Spirit of God to control his life, the Spirit grows His fruit in the believer's life: "love, joy, peace, longsuffering, gentleness, goodness, faith, meekness, temperance [self-control]" (Gal. 5:22–23). These graces do not just spring into being; the Spirit must grow them in the life and character of the believer. The believer must keep on following the Spirit's leading and give Him more and more of his life to control.

PRAYER

Dear Lord, give me the grace to allow the Spirit to control my life and lead me in paths of righteousness. For Jesus' sake. Amen.

MARCH 8

"So he [God] drove out the man; and he placed at the east of the garden of Eden Cherubims, and a flaming sword which turned every way, to keep the way of the tree of life" (Gen. 3:24). At the beginning of mankind's sin God closed the way to the garden of Eden. Man must forsake his sin to find paradise. God has concluded, "There is none righteous, no, not one" (Rom. 3:10). But "Christ Jesus came into the world to save sinners" (1 Tim. 1:15). Jesus Christ is the "one mediator between God and men" (1 Tim. 2:5). "But now in Christ Jesus ye who sometimes were far off are made nigh by the blood of Christ" (Eph. 2:13). "For through him we both have access by one Spirit unto the Father" (Eph. 2:18). Jesus said, "Him that cometh to me I will in no wise cast out" (John 6:37*b*).

PRAYER

Thank You, Lord Jesus, for dying for my sins. Give me the grace to live for You in this wicked world. Amen.

MARCH 9

"**F**or this is he, of whom it is written, Behold, I send my messenger before thy face, which shall prepare thy way before thee" (Matt. 11:10). This verse speaks of the ministry of John the Baptist. He was a great prophet, but his glory was that he prepared the way for the Lord Jesus Christ. Every Christian worker needs to remember that the greatest thing he can do for the Lord is not his personal achievements but preparing the way for the Lord Jesus to work in hearts. We can prepare the ground; we can sow the seed, but it is the Lord alone Who can bring forth the harvest. We are sent forth to be witnesses to Him. He alone is the Savior of all who will believe. Our greatest service is to direct people to Him.

PRAYER

Lord Jesus, help us to be good witnesses for You. Give us the ability to direct men's attention to how great You are. Amen.

MARCH 10

"**A**nd thine ears shall hear a word behind thee, saying, This is the way, walk ye in it, when ye turn to the right hand, and when ye turn to the left" (Isa. 30:21). God guides His people on the pathway of life. The believer must often face adversity, but God always provides leading to help him on a path that honors God. Many times that leading comes through the Holy Scriptures. The believer will remember a verse that illumines the right pathway for him. In reading Scripture the believer may see a verse that seems to glow with special significance. We should always stop to meditate on that verse, for God may be calling to our attention some specific leading for our life. God uses Scripture to guide our pathway to Himself.

PRAYER

O Lord, guide our steps on the path of life, that our steps may honor and please You. For Jesus' sake. Amen.

MARCH 11

"**A**nd an highway shall be there, and a way, and it shall be called The way of holiness; the unclean shall not pass over it; but it shall be for those: the wayfaring men, though fools, shall not err therein" (Isa. 35:8). This is a prophecy of the coming millennial reign of Christ. But believers today also need to walk in the way of holiness, set apart for God. Those who walk with God may not have great mental equipment, but that does not matter. God is all-wise and can lead the believer in the right pathway. The believer must always keep in mind that he is walking with God in this life, on a path that leads to the presence of God in glory. We must learn how to walk with God, not running ahead, and not lagging behind. His presence is the great blessing of our life.

PRAYER

O Lord, help us to walk the way of holiness with You. Keep us mindful of Your presence with us and guide us. For Jesus' sake. Amen.

MARCH 12

"They that wait upon the Lord shall renew their strength; they shall mount up with wings as eagles; they shall run, and not be weary; and they shall walk, and not faint" (Isa. 40:31). The believer's path is often difficult and his strength often weak. Instead of just gritting the teeth and staggering onward, it is better to seek the Lord and wait upon Him. He can uphold the believer and renew his strength. By the grace of God the believer can run without weariness and can keep on walking without fainting. "The eternal God is thy refuge, and underneath are the everlasting arms" (Deut. 33:27*a*). The important thing for the believer is to wait on the Lord. Concentrate on His mighty power and His loving care.

PRAYER

O Lord, sustain us by Your grace and enable us to run our race with patience and determination. For Jesus' sake. Amen.

MARCH 13

"**T**he people that walked in darkness have seen a great light: they that dwell in the land of the shadow of death, upon them hath the light shined" (Isa. 9:2). Matthew quotes this verse as fulfilled in the Galilean ministry of the Lord Jesus Christ (Matt. 4:14–16). Jesus preached, "Repent: for the kingdom of heaven is at hand" (Matt. 4:17). He was not uttering pious platitudes; He was demanding change in thinking and living. Believers must turn their backs on the darkness and walk in the light of the Lord. The wicked world lies in darkness, but the believer can let his light shine for the Lord. He needs to fill his mind with Scripture that his life may count for the Lord. "The righteousness of thy testimonies is everlasting: give me understanding, and I shall live" (Ps. 119:144).

PRAYER

O Lord, let the light of Your Word guide my steps and make me a good witness for You in this wicked world. Amen.

MARCH 14

"The Lord is slow to anger, and great in power, and will not at all acquit the wicked: the Lord hath his way in the whirlwind and in the storm, and the clouds are the dust of his feet" (Nah. 1:3). God's providence guides all things, even the storms. But if God is displeased with man, "who can stand before his indignation?" (Nah. 1:6*a*). Every person needs to be reconciled to God. He is ready to forgive, but man must ask Him for forgiveness. God is listening and is ready to receive those who seek His face. "The Lord is good, a strong hold in the day of trouble; and he knoweth them that trust in him" (Nah. 1:7). God exercises providential care for His people. They should trust in Him, not in their own foresight and skill.

PRAYER

Thank You, Lord, for being a stronghold of safety for Your people. Guide our steps and protect us from harm. For Jesus' sake. Amen.

MARCH 15

"They have refused to receive correction: they have made their faces harder than a rock . . . for they know not the way of the Lord" (Jer. 5:3–4). The prophet writes of the sins of his people, who have not listened to the word of the Lord. The prophet Jeremiah stood in the gate and cried out, "Hear the word of the Lord. . . . Amend your ways" (Jer. 7:2–3). God commanded them, "Obey my voice, and I will be your God, and ye shall be my people: and walk ye in all the ways that I have commanded you, that it may be well unto you. But they hearkened not" (Jer. 7:23–24). People still harden their hearts against the word of the Lord and walk in contrary ways. They will reap the whirlwind, just as the people of Israel did. We all need a submissive heart to listen to the Word of the Lord and to obey.

PRAYER

O Lord, give us an obedient heart to hear Your Word and to obey. Turn us away from sinful paths to walk with You. For Jesus' sake. Amen.

MARCH 16

"There shall be false teachers among you . . . and many shall follow their pernicious ways; by reason of whom the way of truth shall be evil spoken of" (2 Pet. 2:1–2). We live in a day in which many people pose as Bible believers, but they are not. They infiltrate Christian works in order to lead the work astray. Peter warned, "They with feigned words make merchandise of you" (2 Pet. 2:3*b*). They are out for material profit, not the glory of the Lord Jesus Christ. "They themselves are the servants [literally slaves] of corruption" (2 Pet. 2:19*b*). The believer must stand firm for the glory of the Lord Jesus Christ. Believers must always follow the Lord Jesus Christ, not the smooth talking deceivers who would lead us away from the clear teaching of the Bible, the truth of God.

PRAYER

O Lord, protect us from the deceptions of men. Help us to obey the Bible and honor the Lord Jesus Christ. In His name. Amen.

MARCH 17

"**S**o he drove out the man; and he placed at the east of the garden of Eden Cherubims, and a flaming sword which turned every way, to keep the way of the tree of life" (Gen. 3:24). Man who sins is shut out from the tree of life. But God sent His Son, Jesus Christ, into the world to give mankind life. Jesus prayed, "This is life eternal, that they might know thee the only true God, and Jesus Christ, whom thou hast sent" (John 17:3). Jesus is the way, the truth, and the life (John 14:6). Salvation is not a quest for some hidden pathway to God; it is a simple receiving of the Lord Jesus Christ as Savior. He alone can cleanse the life from sin and bring the person to His heavenly Father.

PRAYER

Thank You, Lord Jesus, for dying on the cross for me. Help me to remember that You are the Source of my life. Amen.

MARCH 18

"Now I Nebuchadnezzar praise and extol and honour the King of heaven, all whose works are truth, and his ways judgment: and those that walk in pride he is able to abase" (Dan. 4:37). The mighty king had learned that God could easily remove his power to rule, and even to think. Now the king had repented and walked in humility before God. That is an object lesson that all men should take seriously. Solomon wrote, "A man's pride shall bring him low" (Prov. 29:23). The apostle John warned, "The pride of life is not of the Father, but is of the world" (1 John 2:16). Peter exhorts, "Yea, all of you be subject one to another, and be clothed with humility: for God resisteth the proud, and giveth grace to the humble" (1 Pet. 5:5).

PRAYER

O Lord, help us to walk humbly with You and follow the teaching of Your Word. Give us grace to be obedient and zealous. For Jesus' sake. Amen.

MARCH 19

David asks, "Lord, who shall abide in thy tabernacle? who shall dwell in thy holy hill?" (Ps. 15:1). Then he answers his question, "He that walketh uprightly, and worketh righteousness, and speaketh the truth in his heart" (v. 2). The man who lives his life uprightly shall abide in the tabernacle of the Lord. He is not a person who backbites others (v. 3), but instead he honors them that reverence God (v. 4). He speaks the truth in his heart, and consequently he speaks the truth to others as well. He does not take bribes against the innocent (v. 5). God is holy. The person who wishes to abide in the presence of the Lord must be holy and dedicated to the Lord. No wonder that David could say, "The Lord is the portion of mine inheritance" (Ps. 16:5*a*).

PRAYER

O Lord, help us to abide in Your presence and to walk uprightly in the sight of the world. For Jesus' sake. Amen.

MARCH 20

"**I** will instruct thee and teach thee in the way which thou shalt go: I will guide thee with mine eye" (Ps. 32:8). David's words reveal the voice of God in guiding His people. God does not expect His people to stumble along, groping for the way. God teaches His people through His Word and guides them providentially. David warns the believer against being stubborn, like the horse that must be guided by bit and bridle (v. 9). The believer should seek God's guidance and walk the path joyfully. "He that trusteth in the Lord, mercy shall compass him about" (v. 10*b*). Walking with God is a blessed privilege. David exhorts, "Be glad in the Lord, and rejoice, ye righteous: and shout for joy, all ye that are upright in heart" (v. 11).

PRAYER

Thank You, Lord, for guiding our steps and leading us along the path that leads to our eternal home with You. Amen.

MARCH 21

Samuel said, "God forbid that I should sin against the Lord in ceasing to pray for you: but I will teach you the good and the right way: only fear the Lord, and serve him in truth with all your heart" (1 Sam. 12:23–24). The people had rejected Samuel's rule and had chosen Saul as king instead. Still Samuel was determined to continue praying for them instructing them in the Word of the Lord. He is a good example for all servants of the Lord who may be rejected by those they wish to serve. Samuel continued to serve by praying for them. At times that is the only way we can serve some people. Samuel reverenced the Lord and continued to serve Him with all his heart. That is a path that is open to us all.

PRAYER

O Lord, help us to serve You with all our hearts and to continue praying for those we cannot reach any other way. For Jesus' sake. Amen.

MARCH 22

"**C**ommit thy way unto the Lord; trust also in him; and he shall bring it to pass" (Ps. 37:5). The believer must put the guidance of his life into the hands of the Lord and walk by faith. He cannot see the end, but the Lord can. He should trust in the Lord to bring him out at the right place. The psalmist goes on to say, "Rest in the Lord, and wait patiently for him: fret not thyself because of him who prospereth in his way, because of the man who bringeth wicked devices to pass" (v. 7). The believer should wait on the Lord because the Lord has already planned his deliverance. The Lord can protect His people and bring judgment upon the wicked. "For evildoers shall be cut off: but those that wait upon the Lord, they shall inherit the earth" (Ps. 37:9).

PRAYER

Thank You, Lord, for guiding our steps and protecting our way. Help us to walk in faithful submission to You. For Jesus' sake. Amen.

MARCH 23

Jesus said to His disciples, "I have compassion on the multitude, because they continue with me now three days, and have nothing to eat: and I will not send them away fasting, lest they faint in the way" (Matt. 15:32*b*). The Lord always cared for people. On this occasion the Lord Jesus fed four thousand people with seven loaves and a few little fishes (v. 34). The text records that they took up seven baskets full of the fragments that remained (v. 37). We must always remember that the Lord Jesus cares for us in the same compassionate way. By His grace he will provide for our needs as well. People may forget us, but the Lord never does. Believers ought to have compassion on the poor and needy as the Lord Jesus did.

PRAYER

Thank You, Lord, for Your loving care of Your people. Help us to be mindful of the needs of others as well. For Jesus' sake. Amen.

March 24

"**T**hus saith the Lord, Stand ye in the ways, and see, and ask for the old paths, where is the good way, and walk therein, and ye shall find rest for your souls" (Jer. 6:16). The believer needs old-fashioned devotion to God and obedience to His Word. We need family prayers and family devotions and a daily reading of God's Word to sanctify our homes for the Lord. Modern life is filled with busy activities that lead nowhere, certainly not toward devotion to God and His Word. No one accidentally becomes a true servant of God. Believers must deliberately choose to serve God, to walk in His ways, to read and obey His Word as the faithful believers of old have always done. The way of the Lord leads home.

Prayer

O Lord, help us to make Your Word central in our lives, that we may be a testimony for You in this wicked world. For Jesus' sake. Amen.

MARCH 25

People who refuse to reverence the Lord in their life do so at their own risk. "They despised all my reproof. Therefore shall they eat of the fruit of their own way, and be filled with their own devices" (Prov. 1:30–31). The person who tries to use his own tricks to solve his problems will be caught in them. The devices he tries will be turned against him. There are always consequences. But those who reverence the Lord and walk in His ways will find guidance and blessing from the Lord. Solomon urges, "Incline thine ear unto wisdom, and apply thine heart to understanding" (Prov. 2:2). "Then shalt thou understand the fear of the Lord, and find the knowledge of God" (Prov. 2:5).

PRAYER

O Lord, give us wisdom and help us to walk in reverence to Your will. For Jesus' sake. Amen.

MARCH 26

Jesus said, "If any man walk in the day, he stumbleth not, because he seeth the light of this world. But if a man walk in the night, he stumbleth, because there is no light in him" (John 11:9*b*–10). Spiritual light does not come from some mystical inner self. The light of life comes from God's Word, the Bible. The psalmist wrote, "Thy word is a lamp unto my feet, and a light unto my path" (Ps. 119:105). Everyone needs spiritual illumination on the path of his or her life. The Lord Jesus commanded, "Search the scriptures; for in them ye think ye have eternal life: and they are they which testify of me" (John 5:39). Every believer ought to search the Scriptures daily that he might have light upon his pathway.

PRAYER

Lord Jesus, help us to see You in Scripture and to walk our path in the light of Your Word. Amen.

MARCH 27

"**T**he steps of a good man are ordered by the Lord: and he delighteth in his way" (Ps. 37:23). The good man trusts in the Lord. "Though he fall, he shall not be utterly cast down: for the Lord upholdeth him with his hand" (v. 24). The Lord plans the life of those who trust in Him. The believer should trust in the Lord to uphold him and to enable him to accomplish all that the Lord wills. The believer needs to learn to walk patiently the path that God opens before him. It is not an easy path, but it is always a blessed one. The Lord has a purpose for every believer's life. As the believer walks with God, the Lord fulfills His purpose step by step.

PRAYER

O Lord, guide our steps on the pathway of Your purpose. Enable us to accomplish Your will in our lives. For Jesus' sake. Amen.

MARCH 28

"**T**herefore we are buried with him by baptism into death: that like as Christ was raised up from the dead by the glory of the Father, even so we also should walk in newness of life" (Rom. 6:4). In Scripture to walk is to live the life. The person who trusts Christ for salvation is a new creature in Christ. His life should reflect that inward change in heart and direction. Now he is alive to the things of God through Jesus Christ (Rom. 6:11). Now he rejoices in the worship and service of God. Now, instead of thinking only of himself, he thinks of others. Now he should yield himself as an instrument of God to be a blessing to others (Rom. 6:13). His walk should make manifest to others that he is walking with God.

PRAYER

O Lord, help us to walk with You along the path of life. Give us grace to manifest the new life we have from You. For Jesus' sake. Amen.

MARCH 29

"**F**or the commandment is a lamp; and the law is light; and reproofs of instruction are the way of life" (Prov. 6:23). God's Word is a precious lamp that illuminates the pathway of believers. It often reproves our actions and redirects our steps. We need to search the Scriptures daily so that we may walk our pathway in the light of God's revealed will. To walk in darkness is to invite a fall, but to walk according to God's Word is to walk in the light. No wonder the psalmist prayed, "Open thou mine eyes, that I may behold wondrous things out of thy law" (Ps. 119:18). That is a petition that all believers need to pray for themselves. It is a great blessing to walk the pathway of God's will in the light of His holy Word.

PRAYER

O Lord, lead me in the light of Your Word that I may walk with You on the path of life. For Jesus' sake. Amen.

MARCH 30

"I shall not die but live, and declare the works of the Lord" (Ps. 118:17). In his distress the psalmist called upon the Lord and the Lord answered him (Ps. 118:5). We must all remember to turn to the Lord in times of trouble. The psalmist was sure that the Lord heard him and would answer his prayer. We, too, must pray in faith, expecting the Lord to hear and to answer according to His perfect will. The psalmist had many enemies who desired to slay him, but he was sure that God was much more powerful than his enemies were. He could declare the works of the Lord with the confidence that the Lord was still at work, and would accomplish his purpose through the psalmist. That must be our faith as well.

PRAYER

O Lord, hear our cries for help and protection. Let your presence be our defense and our blessing. For Jesus' sake. Amen.

MARCH 31

"**F**or this God is our God for ever and ever: he will be our guide even unto death" (Ps. 48:14). The holy God of Scripture is our God forever and forever. He does not allow His people to wander aimlessly; He guides them through life to fulfill His purpose. His purpose for them does not end with this life. He will guide them throughout eternity future. He has an eternal purpose for all His people that only He knows. It will be one of the joys of heaven to learn all that He has planned for the future service of His people. We have thought of the loving-kindness of our God, but we will have much more to think about when the vistas of heaven open before us.

PRAYER

O Lord, help us to follow Your leading here and give us the faith to follow Your leading all the way home to Your presence in glory. For Jesus' sake. Amen.

APRIL 1

"**F**or he shall give his angels charge over thee, to keep thee in all thy ways" (Ps. 91:11). The Bible clearly teaches that there is a ministry of guardian angels over God's people. "Surely he shall deliver thee from the snare of the fowler, and from the noisome pestilence" (Ps. 91:3). God can thwart the tricks of evil men and preserve the steps of His people on His pathway for their lives. God's people must learn to look to the Lord for help in times of trouble. God promises, "He shall call upon me, and I will answer him: I will be with him in trouble; I will deliver him, and honour him. With long life will I satisfy him, and shew him my salvation" (Ps. 91:15–16).

PRAYER

Thank You, Lord, for protecting our pathway and for delivering us from countless trials and snares. Help us to walk with You. For Jesus' sake. Amen.

APRIL 2

The prophet Isaiah proclaimed the word of the Lord, "I will even make a way in the wilderness, and rivers in the desert" (Isa. 43:19). This prophecy was fulfilled in the ministry of John the Baptist, when he came "preaching in the wilderness of Judaea, and saying, Repent ye: for the kingdom of heaven is at hand" (Matt. 3:1–2). The inhabitants of Jerusalem and all Judaea went out to hear the preaching of a great prophet. John was the first prophet in four centuries to proclaim the word of the Lord. His message of repentance is still appropriate. People should repent of their sins and turn to the Lord for forgiveness. John was the forerunner of the Lord Jesus Christ, the only One Who can save from sin. Jesus promised, "I am the good shepherd: the good shepherd giveth his life for the sheep" (John 10:11).

PRAYER

Thank You, Lord Jesus, for dying for my sins; give me grace to follow You wherever You lead. Amen.

APRIL 3

"**W**e do not cease to pray for you. . . . That ye might walk worthy of the Lord unto all pleasing, being fruitful in every good work, and increasing in the knowledge of God" (Col. 1:9–10). Paul never stopped praying for others; too often we "sign off." Paul continued praying that other believers might demonstrate a life worthy of the Lord Jesus. Believers should continue living lives that are fruitful in the Lord's work. All believers should continually search the Scriptures that their knowledge of God might constantly increase. Knowledge of the Scriptures enlarges our understanding of God and His will for our lives. We should continue praying that our lives may bear fruit for Him.

PRAYER

O Lord, make us fruitful believers, constantly increasing in our knowledge of You and service for You. In Jesus' name. Amen.

APRIL 4

The Lord God said concerning Abraham, "For I know him, that he will command his children and his household after him, and they shall keep the way of the Lord, to do justice and judgment" (Gen. 18:19). Abraham believed in, and obeyed, the Lord. God rescued Lot and his family because of Abraham's intercession (Gen. 19). Yet judgment fell on wicked Sodom. Every believer should recognize that God is watching his household also. Does the household honor God? Is there daily Bible reading and prayer? God knew the character of Abraham. So He knows the character of every professing believer. No one can fool God. David vowed, "I will walk within my house with a perfect heart" (Ps. 101:2).

PRAYER

O Lord, help us to honor You in our hearts and in our homes. Give us grace to live our lives in Your presence. For Jesus' sake. Amen.

APRIL 5

"**F**or ye are yet carnal: for whereas there is among you envying, and strife, and divisions, are ye not carnal, and walk as men?" (1 Cor. 3:3). Unfortunately a worldly spirit often characterizes believers. Paul here rebukes believers for fleshly attitudes that hurt their testimony. Envying and strife and divisions can still be found in churches. We all need to remember Paul's words: "For we are labourers together with God: ye are God's husbandry, ye are God's building" (1 Cor. 3:9). Believers need to learn to work together to accomplish God's will. Each believer is just a part of His building. We all need to learn how to fit together into the church, which is His building, not just ours.

PRAYER

Dear Lord, give us a sweet spirit of love and cooperation in Your house that we may be a blessing to others and an honor to You. For Jesus' sake. Amen.

April 6

Wisdom cries out: "Now therefore hearken unto me, O ye children: for blessed are they that keep my ways. . . . Blessed is the man that heareth me, watching daily at my gates. . . . For whoso findeth me findeth life, and shall obtain favour of the Lord" (Prov. 8:32, 34*a*, 35). Everyone will admit that he needs wisdom, but few people ask the Lord for it. Wise people will seek the Lord and His Word for guidance. The fool rushes to the precipice and plunges over. Those who walk according to the wisdom of Scripture will have peace of mind and the sense of the Lord's presence with them. The Lord is infinitely wise and delights in imparting His wisdom to His people.

Prayer

O Lord, grant us Your wisdom and guide our steps according to Your Word that our path may please You. For Jesus' sake. Amen.

APRIL 7

"**A**nd it came to pass, when Pharaoh had let the people go, that God led them not through the way of the land of the Philistines, although that was near; for God said, Lest peradventure the people repent when they see war, and they return to Egypt: but God led the people about, through the way of the wilderness of the Red sea" (Exod. 13:17–18*a*). The way through the wilderness may seem hard for believers, but God knows that the alternative would be much more dangerous. Believers must always remember that although their path seems hard, God chooses the best path for them and the path that will bring them safely to His place for them. God always chooses the very best for His people.

PRAYER

Thank You, Lord, for guiding us through the difficulties of life. Help us to see Your providential care for Your people. For Jesus' sake. Amen.

APRIL 8

Referring to Apollos Scripture says, "This man was instructed in the way of the Lord; and being fervent in the spirit, he spake and taught diligently the things of the Lord, knowing only the baptism of John" (Acts 18:25). Aquila and Priscilla "took him unto them, and expounded unto him the way of God more perfectly" (Acts 18:26). This is a lovely example of Christian kindness. Instead of denouncing his errors publicly, Aquila and Priscilla quietly explained the truth about Christ to him. The result was that he became one of the most powerful Christian preachers. We can all learn that the path of quiet kindness is the best way to correct the errors of others.

PRAYER

Dear Lord, give us the spirit of sympathetic kindness that we may be able to help others to serve You well. For Jesus' sake. Amen.

APRIL 9

King Saul claimed, "Yea, I have obeyed the voice of the Lord, and have gone the way which the Lord sent me, and have brought Agag the king of Amalek" (1 Sam. 15:20). But Saul had not obeyed the Lord, and the prophet Samuel responded, "Hath the Lord as great delight in burnt offerings and sacrifices, as in obeying the voice of the Lord? Behold, to obey is better than sacrifice" (v. 22). People will regularly offer the Lord something they want rather than to simply obey what the Lord has revealed. Samuel pronounced a divine judgment against Saul: "Because thou hast rejected the word of the Lord, he hath also rejected thee from being king" (1 Sam. 15:23). Obedience is the very best way to show that you believe.

PRAYER

Dear Lord, help us to obey your Word and to walk humbly with You. Amen.

April 10

"**O**h that my people had hearkened unto me, and Israel had walked in my ways!" (Ps. 81:13). Israel had called upon God for help, and God had delivered them (v. 7). But now Israel would not listen to God's word (v. 11). God was ready to deliver them, but they would not ask (v. 14). All too often God's people struggle along in grave difficulties but do not ask the Lord for deliverance. God is ready to satisfy His people with honey out of the rock, but they will not ask (v. 16). We need to ask the Lord for help and deliverance. We need to look to the Lord for wisdom and guidance. He is able to lead His people safely through the wilderness and bring them to the place of blessing and safety.

Prayer

O Lord, deliver us from our self-sufficiency. Bring us near to You and help us to seek Your face in all things. For Jesus' sake. Amen.

APRIL 11

Paul speaks of Abraham, forefather of the Jewish people, and of all who share the faith of Abraham. "And the father of circumcision to them who are not of the circumcision only, but who also walk in the steps of that faith of our father Abraham, which he had being yet uncircumcised" (Rom. 4:12). Ritual ceremonies do not make a person right with God; there must be faith in the revealed Word of God. Abraham took God at His word; today we also need to take God at His word and trust that word for our life and our salvation. Abraham "was strong in faith, giving glory to God" (Rom. 4:20*b*). Paul concludes, "Therefore being justified by faith, we have peace with God through our Lord Jesus Christ" (Rom. 5:1).

PRAYER

O Lord, give us grace to trust in Your Word of salvation through the Lord Jesus Christ and enable us to walk with You by faith. Amen.

APRIL 12

"**W**ait on the Lord, and keep his way, and he shall exalt thee to inherit the land: when the wicked are cut off, thou shalt see it" (Ps. 37:34). Waiting on the Lord means ordering the life in obedience to the Lord's will. To keep his way is to live the life in conformity to God's revealed Word. The wicked, who spurn God's Word, will find out that there are always consequences to transgressing His Word. The believer who waits on the Lord will learn that God honors those who obey His Word. He will also see that the wicked, who live for material things, will leave all they have and pass into another realm that they are not prepared to face. Waiting on the Lord is not a waste of time but a preparation for eternity.

PRAYER

O Lord, help us to walk with You in the light of Your Word and to wait on Your will in all things. For Jesus' sake. Amen.

APRIL 13

Paul exhorts, "Nevertheless, whereto we have already attained, let us walk by the same rule, let us mind the same thing" (Phil. 3:16). Paul knew that it was necessary for believers to maintain a steady, consistent life in the sight of God. So we must all live consistent lives as a testimony to the grace of Christ. But Paul had great zeal for the service of Christ as well. "I press toward the mark for the prize of the high calling of God in Christ Jesus" (Phil. 3:14). We, too, need zeal for the service of Christ, but we must never let our enthusiasm cause us to forget the daily, humble walk with Christ. Devotion to Christ ought to be supreme in every Christian's life. Zeal is never a substitute for devotion. They belong together in the Christian's heart.

PRAYER

Dear Lord, help us to walk with You every day. Give us the zeal to serve you with devotion and faithfulness. For Jesus' sake. Amen.

APRIL 14

"**F**or thou hast delivered my soul from death: wilt not thou deliver my feet from falling, that I may walk before God in the light of the living?" (Ps. 56:13). David praised God for delivering him from the attack of the Philistines. He was sure that God had saved his life for a purpose, that he might live as a testimony for God in the land of the living. He was sure that God would deliver his feet from falling. Every believer should live his life in that same faith that God will preserve him so that he may be a testimony for God in the land of the living. We must walk by faith that God will use us as a testimony of His grace to those who know us. Our lives should proclaim to all that we know Jesus Christ as Savior.

PRAYER

Dear Lord, help us so to live that people will know that we belong to You. Preserve our steps for Your glory. For Jesus' sake. Amen.

APRIL 15

"Therefore shall ye lay up these my words in your heart and in your soul. . . . And ye shall teach them your children, speaking of them when thou sittest in thine house, and when thou walkest by the way, when thou liest down, and when thou risest up" (Deut. 11:18–19). Families can talk about anything and everything in their homes, but it is sometimes rare that they talk about God's Word. God here commands His people to make His Word a subject of daily conversation. God's Word ought to guide and control every believer's life. It is only natural that believers should talk about such an important guide. If children grow up never hearing their parents talk about the Bible, they will naturally conclude that it is not an important book.

PRAYER

Dear Lord, help us to digest and absorb Your Holy Bible and to talk about it, that it may guide our daily lives. For Jesus' sake. Amen.

APRIL 16

"**F**or if ye shall diligently keep all these commandments which I command you, to do them, to love the Lord your God, to walk in all his ways, and to cleave unto him; then will the Lord drive out all these nations from before you" (Deut. 11:22–23*a*). We all know that the Israelites did not keep the commandments of the Lord, and He did not drive the hostile nations out for them. But this is a standing warning to all God's people that obedience to His Word is the key to God's blessing. We all need to center our lives on Scripture and to let it guide our lives. If we truly love the Lord our God, we will want to please Him and to walk His pathway. That is always the way of blessing for God's people.

PRAYER

Dear Lord, give us grace to walk the path of life with You and to seek to please You every day. For Jesus' sake. Amen.

APRIL 17

It was Paul's testimony: "I am crucified with Christ: nevertheless I live; yet not I, but Christ liveth in me: and the life which I now live in the flesh I live by the faith of the Son of God, who loved me, and gave himself for me" (Gal. 2:20). Every believer needs this kind of dedication to Christ. Paul did not choose how to serve the Lord Jesus; he let the Lord choose for him. He simply obeyed the Lord and went where He sent him. The result was a harvest of souls for Christ all over the ancient world. Christ always gives His very best to those who leave the choice to Him. Believers still need to sacrifice their own desires that Christ may live through them and manifest His love today.

PRAYER

Dear Lord, help me to forget myself and use me to be a blessing to others this day. For Jesus' sake. Amen.

April 18

"The way of the Lord is strength to the upright: but destruction shall be to the workers of iniquity" (Prov. 10:29). People who follow the will of the Lord find that His strength upholds them. On the other hand, those who are workers of iniquity and sin will always find that there are continuing consequences to their deeds. It may take some time, but retribution will find them.

Prayer

Dear Lord, keep us on the right path of Your will and protect us from the destructive path of the wicked. For Jesus' sake. Amen.

APRIL 19

The apostle Paul exhorts believers, "See then that ye walk circumspectly, not as fools, but as wise, redeeming the time, because the days are evil" (Eph. 5:15–16). To walk circumspectly is to walk with great caution. Picture an ancient stone wall with the top of it set with sharp rocks, jagged metal, and broken glass in concrete. Now picture a cat walking along that wall, carefully placing each paw between the sharp projections. That is the picture Paul gives for us to follow. The believer should not plunge into disaster, but he should live his life with great caution, watching his steps that they honor the Lord. We need to buy back the time, for we get a chance to live our life only once.

PRAYER

Dear Lord, help us to live for You. Keep our steps from falling and grant that our lives may count for You. For Jesus' sake. Amen.

APRIL 20

"**T**hus saith the Lord, thy Redeemer, the Holy One of Israel; I am the Lord thy God which teacheth thee to profit, which leadeth thee by the way that thou shouldest go. O that thou hadst hearkened to my commandments!" (Isa. 48:17–18*a*). The Lord God here rebuked His ancient people. He had led them in the ways of righteousness, but they had not followed. He had chosen them in the furnace of affliction (v. 10), but they had not obeyed Him. He reminded them that they had not listened to His commandments. If they would just listen to Him, "then had thy peace been as a river" (v. 18*b*). But now they would have to flee from the Chaldeans (v. 20). "There is no peace, saith the Lord, unto the wicked" (v. 22).

PRAYER

O Lord, give us grace to walk with You. Turn away our steps from worldliness, and grant us Your peace. For Jesus' sake. Amen.

APRIL 21

Solomon warned his son against evil companions. "My son, walk not thou in the way with them; refrain thy foot from their path: for their feet run to evil, and make haste to shed blood" (Prov. 1:15–16). The wrong kind of friends can influence a person to do things he would never do by himself. The right relationship with God is far more important than any friendship. "The fear of the Lord is the beginning of knowledge: but fools despise wisdom and instruction" (Prov. 1:7). The believer must learn to live his life according to the teaching of God's holy Word and not to be influenced by false friendship or peer pressure. The favor of God is vastly more valuable than the friendship of any person.

PRAYER

O Lord, help us to walk humbly with You and not to be influenced by those who spurn Your Word. For Jesus' sake. Amen.

April 22

The Lord promised Moses, "Behold, I send an Angel before thee, to keep thee in the way, and to bring thee into the place which I have prepared" (Exod. 23:20). God did not expect the Israelites to conquer the land in their own strength. God's grace and power were needed just as the believer today needs the grace and strength of the Lord in order to live for Him. In spiritual matters self confidence leads to catastrophe. The Lord promised the Israelites, "For mine Angel shall go before thee, and bring thee in unto the Amorites, and the Hittites, and the Perizzites" (Exod. 23:23). The Angel would defeat the enemies and the Israelites would conquer the land. Believers today need the same faith that God will establish them and win their battles.

PRAYER

O Lord, prepare the way for us and lead us into the place of service and blessing by Your grace. For Jesus' sake. Amen.

APRIL 23

Asaph sang the word of the Lord, "Oh that my people had hearkened unto me, and Israel had walked in my ways! I should soon have subdued their enemies" (Ps. 81:13–14*a*). The Lord mourned that His people had turned away from Him and had forgotten their deliverance from the bondage of Egypt (vv. 10–11). If only the people of God had listened to the rebuke of the Lord and had returned to Him, He would have delivered them. The Lord said, "I am the Lord thy God, which brought thee out of the land of Egypt: open thy mouth wide, and I will fill it" (v. 10). Unfortunately, God's people often do not ask much of the Lord and then wonder why they do not receive much from Him. The Lord Jesus urged, "Ask, and it shall be given you" (Matt. 7:7*a*).

PRAYER

O Lord, we are a needy people. Have mercy upon us and hear our prayers for Your grace and help. For Jesus' sake. Amen.

April 24

"**I**f thou shalt keep all these commandments to do them, which I command thee this day, to love the Lord thy God, and to walk ever in his ways; then shalt thou add three cities more for thee, beside these three" (Deut. 19:9). The Lord provided cities of refuge for the Israelites so that a person guilty of accidental manslaughter could flee to them and be safe from execution. If the Israelites were obedient, the Lord promised to add three more such cities on the other side of Jordan. The Lord always responds to the obedience and service of His people. We all ought to be thinking of ways of pleasing the Lord so that His hand of blessing may rest upon us.

PRAYER

Dear Lord, help us to walk in Your ways, that Your hand of blessing may rest upon us. For Jesus' sake. Amen.

APRIL 25

"**T**hus saith the Lord, Learn not the way of the heathen, and be not dismayed at the signs of heaven; for the heathen are dismayed at them" (Jer. 10:2). The believer must live for God in the midst of a lost and perishing generation. He must not let the sinful practices of unsaved people rub off on him. His walk for God must be clear. Superstitious people often fear cloud formations or storms. The believer must trust in the Lord of heaven and earth to sustain him. No believer ever dies until it is time for the Lord to take him home. "Thou wilt keep him in perfect peace, whose mind is stayed on thee: because he trusteth in thee. Trust ye in the Lord for ever: for in the Lord Jehovah is everlasting strength" (Isa. 26:3).

PRAYER

Thank You, Lord, for Your protection and sustaining grace. Help me to live in serene trust in Your protecting hand. For Jesus' sake. Amen.

APRIL 26

David charged Solomon his son, "Be thou strong therefore, and shew thyself a man; and keep the charge of the Lord thy God, to walk in his ways, to keep his statutes" (1 Kings 2:2*b*–3*a*). As long as Solomon walked in the ways of the Lord, he had God's blessing upon his life. All believers need to recognize the necessity of walking with God in their daily lives. The sense of the presence of God is a protection from worry and temptation. If God is with you, how can you worry? We all need the serenity that God's presence brings into our lives. Believers can talk to the Lord about any problem or danger that may arise. The believer's walk leads home.

PRAYER

Dear God, give us grace to walk with You on our daily path. May Your presence be a blessing all the day. For Jesus' sake. Amen.

APRIL 27

"**A**ll we like sheep have gone astray; we have turned every one to his own way; and the Lord hath laid on him the iniquity of us all" (Isa. 53:6). All mankind has turned aside from God's way to their own way of sin and selfishness. But God laid upon His Son, the Lord Jesus Christ, the iniquity of us all. Isaiah prophesied all this ahead of time. "But he was wounded for our transgressions, he was bruised for our iniquities: the chastisement of our peace was upon him; and with his stripes we are healed" (Isa. 53:5). We need to forsake our selfish way and turn to Him for forgiveness and cleansing from sin. "For whosoever shall call upon the name of the Lord shall be saved" (Rom. 10:13).

PRAYER

Dear Lord, forgive our waywardness and cleanse us from our sin. For Jesus' sake. Amen.

APRIL 28

"**A**nd thine ears shall hear a word behind thee, saying, This is the way, walk ye in it, when ye turn to the right hand, and when ye turn to the left" (Isa. 30:21). The Lord promised His people guidance in times of adversity. This is now fulfilled in the ministry of the Holy Spirit, Who indwells believers. The Lord Jesus promised, "Howbeit when he, the Spirit of truth, is come, he will guide you into all truth: for he shall not speak of himself; but whatsoever he shall hear, that shall he speak: and he will shew you things to come" (John 16:13). Believers today should live their lives in submission to the revealed Word of God, the Bible, but there is a real ministry of guidance in the presence of God's Holy Spirit.

PRAYER

Dear Lord, help us to live according to Your Word, the Bible. And help us to follow the leading of Your Holy Spirit day by day. For Jesus' sake. Amen.

April 29

"The righteousness of the perfect shall direct his way: but the wicked shall fall by his own wickedness" (Prov. 11:5). The life of those who are right with God will naturally lead them to paths of blessing and service for God. But the path of the wicked will lead them deeper and deeper into sin and trouble. There are always consequences for a person's actions. Those who love God will find His blessing on their pathway, but those who love wickedness will find their pathway harder and harder to travel. Getting right with God changes the whole direction of a person's walk. Walking the pathway with God means joy and peace, whatever the circumstances. Walking away from Him means disaster and sorrow.

Prayer

Dear Lord, guide my steps that I may walk with You and be a blessing to others. Keep me from stumbling. For Jesus' sake. Amen.

April 30

"**W**herefore lift up the hands which hang down, and the feeble knees; and make straight paths for your feet, lest that which is lame be turned out of the way; but let it rather be healed" (Heb. 12:12–13). It is all too easy for the believer to get discouraged in his Christian life and to be tempted to give up the fight he is engaged in. But to live the Christian life is never easy. There are always adversaries and snares from the Devil to avoid. We must remember that the Lord Jesus Christ met the Devil on the mount of temptation and soundly defeated him (Matt. 4:1–11). We face a defeated enemy, and by the grace of the Lord Jesus Christ, we shall see him defeated again.

Prayer

Lord Jesus, give me grace to let You defeat the Devil again in my life. Strengthen me to live for You. Amen.

MAY 1

"**D**epart from evil, and do good; seek peace, and pursue it" (Ps. 34:14). The writer to the Hebrews refers to this passage when he writes, "Follow peace with all men, and holiness, without which no man shall see the Lord" (Heb. 12:14). The believer must walk through a wicked world, surrounded with temptations. He must have a determined purpose of following the Lord and resisting temptation. "There is no peace, saith the Lord, unto the wicked" (Isa. 48:22). They must be reconciled to God before they can have peace. "But the fruit of the Spirit is love, joy, peace, longsuffering, gentleness, goodness, faith, meekness, temperance: against such there is no law" (Gal. 5:22–23).

PRAYER

Dear Lord, let Your peace rest upon me as I seek to walk with You in this wicked world. May Your Spirit sustain me. For Jesus' sake. Amen.

MAY 2

"Blessed are they that keep his testimonies, and that seek him with the whole heart. They also do no iniquity: they walk in his ways" (Ps. 119:2–3). God's blessing rests upon the people who sincerely seek Him. To walk in the ways of the Lord means to order one's life according to the teaching of Scripture. Obeying God's Word preserves a person from sin. It also provides blessed fellowship with God. God and the believer can walk together on a holy pathway. The believer should always be concerned that his life match the teaching of Scripture. The psalmist declared, "Thy word have I hid in mine heart, that I might not sin against thee" (Ps. 119:11).

PRAYER

Dear Lord, help me to walk with You. Guide my steps in pathways of service and blessing. Keep me conscious of Your presence. Amen.

MAY 3

"Let the wicked forsake his way, and the unrighteous man his thoughts: and let him return unto the Lord, and he will have mercy upon him; and to our God, for he will abundantly pardon" (Isa. 55:7). A person who is not right with God can get right with Him by turning away from his sin and asking God for pardon and forgiveness. God is gracious to the unworthy and forgiving to the repentant. People are not so forgiving toward those who have wronged them, but God is infinitely compassionate toward those who repent and turn to Him for forgiveness. God gathers the outcasts of Israel (Isa. 56:8). "For thy mercy is great unto the heavens" (Ps. 57:10).

PRAYER

O Lord, forgive my sins, and restore me to Your fellowship. Give me grace to live for You. For Jesus' sake. Amen.

MAY 4

"**B**ut when divers were hardened, and believed not, but spake evil of that way before the multitude, he [Paul] departed from them, and separated the disciples, disputing daily in the school of one Tyrannus" (Acts 19:9). When opposition to the gospel arose, the apostle Paul was quick to adopt new methods. School buildings were not used in the heat of the afternoon, so Paul utilized one of these buildings to preach and teach believers. Today believers often need to be innovative in beginning a new church work. Methods can vary, but the truth of the gospel is unchanging and powerful. The Lord Jesus Christ is the Savior of all who will believe.

PRAYER

Dear Lord, help Your people to continue preaching the good news of salvation through the shed blood of the Lord Jesus Christ. Amen.

MAY 5

"**I** will recompense thee according to thy ways and thine abominations that are in the midst of thee; and ye shall know that I am the Lord that smiteth" (Ezek. 7:9*b*). The Lord solemnly warned His people of impending judgment. He had borne their sinful deeds, but judgment was now coming. In our own day people go on their way heedless of the will of God, but there will be a day of accounting. The Lord said, "Let not the buyer rejoice, nor the seller mourn: for wrath is upon all the multitude thereof" (Ezek. 7:12*b*). People in our own generation need to get right with God for judgment will come on the sins of any people. "Their silver and their gold shall not be able to deliver them in the day of the wrath of the Lord" (Ezek. 7:19*b*).

PRAYER

O Lord, have mercy on Your people, and help us to walk with You in the midst of a wicked and sinful people. For Jesus' sake. Amen.

MAY 6

"**R**ighteousness keepeth him that is upright in the way: but wickedness overthroweth the sinner" (Prov. 13:6). Righteousness guards the steps of the upright person. The sinner confidently assumes that he will get away with his wickedness, but that very wickedness will ultimately throw him down. "Evil pursueth sinners: but to the righteous good shall be repayed" (Prov. 13:21). There is a God in heaven Who blesses the righteous and brings judgment upon the wicked. It is the privilege of God's children to walk humbly with Him on their pilgrim pathway. His way leads to a blessed home.

PRAYER

Dear Lord, help us to walk with You on this pilgrim pathway. Guard our steps and bring us safely home. For Jesus' sake. Amen.

MAY 7

"**F**or the Lord God is a sun and shield: the Lord will give grace and glory: no good thing will he withhold from them that walk uprightly" (Ps. 84:11). To walk uprightly is to live the life according to God's Word, pleasing in His sight. In the ancient world the sun was the greatest blessing. If the sun does not shine, there will be no crops. If God does not "shine" upon His people, there will be no blessing. But God is also a protection from the assaults of enemies and circumstances. God also gives grace and glory to His people. He daily pours out good things upon His people. We need to remember His blessings with thanksgiving.

PRAYER

O Lord, shine upon us with Your grace and enable us to walk pleasing to You through this wicked world. For Jesus' sake. Amen.

MAY 8

"**W**hen thou saidst, Seek ye my face; my heart said unto thee, Thy face, Lord, will I seek" (Ps. 27:8). The direction of the believer's life must be toward God. That means that he must turn his back on the world and its blandishments. David regarded the Lord as his light (v. 1). The believer must seek the Lord in the light of His Word. David prayed, "Hide not thy face far from me; put not thy servant away in anger: thou hast been my help; leave me not, neither forsake me, O God of my salvation" (v. 9). David sought the Lord with all his heart. We, too, need to seek the Lord through His Word by searching the Scriptures daily. He that seeks the Lord shall surely find Him.

PRAYER

O Lord, guide me through Your Word that I may seek You and find You in Your holy Word. For Jesus' sake. Amen.

MAY 9

"God be merciful unto us, and bless us; and cause his face to shine upon us; Selah. That thy way may be known upon earth" (Ps. 67:1–2). All believers need God's merciful blessing. If His face shines upon His people, it causes His way to become recognized on the earth. We pray for His blessing, not just for ourselves but so that other people may recognize how great the Lord is. "Let the people praise thee, O God; let all the people praise thee" (v. 3). We look forward to the day in which all nations will join in the worship of the true God. "O let the nations be glad and sing for joy: for thou shalt judge the people righteously, and govern the nations upon earth. Selah" (v. 4).

PRAYER

Dear Lord, we praise You for Your goodness and mercy. Hasten the day in which all nations will praise You. For Jesus' sake. Amen.

MAY 10

"The Lord saith, Because they have forsaken my law which I set before them, and have not obeyed my voice, neither walked therein; but have walked after the imagination of their own heart. . . . Therefore thus saith the Lord of hosts, the God of Israel; Behold, I will feed them, even this people, with wormwood" (Jer. 9:13–15). There are always divine consequences for disobeying God's holy Word. Sinners find out that the sin they thought was so attractive turns out to be as bitter as gall. Instead of glorying in their sin, sinners need to repent and forsake their sin. The Lord exhorts, "But let him that glorieth glory in this, that he understandeth and knoweth me, that I am the Lord which exercise lovingkindness, judgment, and righteousness, in the earth" (Jer. 9:24).

PRAYER

Dear Lord, forgive us our sins and failures and help us to walk with You through this wicked world. For Jesus' sake. Amen.

MAY 11

"**D**eliver my soul from the wicked, which is thy sword: from men which are thy hand, O Lord, from men of the world, which have their portion in this life" (Ps. 17:13–14). David prayed for deliverance from the wicked. He reminds us, however, that all the good that wicked people will ever see, they see in this life. The judgment of God awaits them in the next. But God does care for His people in this life as well as in the next. David prayed, "Hold up my goings in thy paths, that my footsteps slip not" (Ps. 17:5). He trusted in God's providential care. But he also trusted in God's loving care in the next as well. "As for me, I will behold thy face in righteousness: I shall be satisfied, when I awake, with thy likeness" (Ps. 17:15).

PRAYER

Dear Lord, protect us from the snares of the wicked in this life and by Your grace bring us into Your presence in the next. For Jesus' sake. Amen.

MAY 12

"**S**urely goodness and mercy shall follow me all the days of my life: and I will dwell in the house of the Lord for ever" (Ps. 23:6). David's trust in the Lord came from a life of experience of the loving kindness of God. He knew that the Lord would never desert him. He trusted in the Lord to provide a place for him in the presence of the Lord forever. Every one of us needs that same assurance of the keeping power of God. If the Lord is our Shepherd, we can follow His leading in the confidence that He knows the best pathway for us and has the power to bring us safely into his presence. Heaven is not just a vocabulary word to believers. It is a very real place that He is preparing for us.

PRAYER

Thank You, Lord, for Your tender loving care. Guide our pathway to that place You have prepared for us. For Jesus' sake. Amen.

MAY 13

"**T**he king shall mourn, and the prince shall be clothed with desolation, and the hands of the people of the land shall be troubled: I will do unto them after their way, and according to their deserts will I judge them; and they shall know that I am the Lord" (Ezek. 7:27). The Lord solemnly declares judgment upon the land, from the highest rulers to the common people. They have despised His Word and now must pay the consequences. In our own day God's people need to beg God for mercy. From the highest levels of government to the lowest levels of street crime, sin and wickedness are rampant. We need to seek revival in our own hearts and reform in the affairs of society and government.

PRAYER

O Lord, have mercy upon us. Turn back the tide of wickedness in our land and revive the hearts of Your people. For Jesus' sake. Amen.

MAY 14

"**O** Lord, I know that the way of man is not in himself: it is not in man that walketh to direct his steps" (Jer. 10:23). The prophet recognized that man does not have the wisdom to successfully guide himself. It is all too easy to take the wrong step. So he prayed, "O Lord, correct me, but with judgment; not in thine anger, lest thou bring me to nothing" (Jer. 10:24). Thus he prays that God correct him, but not with stern judgment. We all need the merciful kindness of God. The Lord with loving care guides His people along the path of life. We must follow in humble obedience to His leading. His Word, the Bible, is the light that illuminates our pathway. We all need to search the Scriptures to find the light of God on our pathway.

PRAYER

Thank You, Lord, for guiding our steps. Illuminate our pathway by Your Word and lead us along the path of life. For Jesus' sake. Amen.

MAY 15

"Lead me in thy truth, and teach me: for thou art the God of my salvation; on thee do I wait all the day" (Ps. 25:5). God leads His people through the truth of His Word. Through the Scriptures we can understand the right pathway to take in this life. We need to wait, that is, to depend on God for guidance along our pathway. His Word can teach us the right way of service and blessing. To stumble blindly forward is to invite disaster. His Word should guide our steps. His wisdom should direct our hearts. We can walk His pathway in peace of mind when His Word directs our steps. Following the leading of His Word always leads us to the right pathway.

PRAYER

O Lord, lead me in the right pathway. Help me to see in Your Word the guidance that I need day by day. For Jesus' sake. Amen.

MAY 16

"**F**or thou art my rock and my fortress; therefore for thy name's sake lead me, and guide me" (Ps. 31:3). The psalmist had put his trust in the Lord (v. 1) and now claimed God as his protection and guide. He noted that his enemies had laid a net to ensnare him (v. 4), but he was sure that the Lord was able to deliver him. The Lord is able to guide His people through all the snares and temptations of life. His Word provides the guidance and strength we need. David said, "I am forgotten as a dead man out of mind: I am like a broken vessel" (v. 12). But he was quick to express his faith in the Lord. "But I trusted in thee, O Lord: I said, Thou art my God" (v. 14). We, too, must be quick to claim the Lord as our deliverer.

PRAYER

O Lord, we need Your strength and deliverance. Extend Your hand of mercy to us, and guide us on Your pathway. For Jesus' sake. Amen.

MAY 17

"**A**nd Jesus going up to Jerusalem took the twelve disciples apart in the way, and said to them, Behold, we go up to Jerusalem: and the Son of man shall be betrayed unto the chief priests and unto the scribes, and they shall condemn him to death" (Matt. 20:17–18). The Lord Jesus took His disciples aside in the way to Jerusalem and explained to them the suffering that He would go through. There is often much that the believer has to suffer in the way of God's path for him. Suffering in the path of God's will strengthens and purifies the believer. No believer ever suffers alone. The Lord is with him every step of the way. When He is through, we shall come forth as gold.

PRAYER

Dear Lord, give us grace to bear the trials and suffering of our path. Help us to sense Your presence with us in every trial. For Jesus' sake. Amen.

MAY 18

"**A**nd, behold, two blind men sitting by the way side, when they heard that Jesus passed by, cried out, saying, Have mercy on us, O Lord, thou son of David" (Matt. 20:30). Although the people told him to keep quiet, the Lord Jesus commanded one of them to be called (Mark 10:49). He was there, not in utter hopelessness as he thought but simply waiting for the Lord's timing. The Lord Jesus healed them both with a simple touch (Matt. 20:34). Believers must not despair in times of affliction. The Lord Jesus is able to meet every need of the human heart. We must wait, however, for His timing. "What time I am afraid, I will trust in thee . . . in God I have put my trust" (Ps. 56:3–4).

PRAYER

Dear Lord, help us to keep on trusting in You. Bring Your deliverance to us in Your own good time. For Jesus' sake. Amen.

MAY 19

"**D**epart from me, ye evildoers: for I will keep the commandments of my God" (Ps. 119:115). The psalmist was committed to serving God with all his heart. Too many believers today "go along" with unbelievers just in order to be pleasant. The psalmist wished to please God above all things. What the enemies of God thought of him did not matter to him. The believer of today must have a devotion to God that is incorruptible. God is more important than the opinions of wicked people. The apostle Paul solemnly declared, "But as we were allowed of God to be put in trust with the gospel, even so we speak; not as pleasing men, but God, which trieth our hearts" (1 Thess. 2:4).

PRAYER

Dear Lord, help us to please You in our daily walk and testimony. Give us the boldness to live for You alone. For Jesus' sake. Amen.

MAY 20

The high priest is one "who can have compassion on the ignorant, and on them that are out of the way; for that he himself also is compassed with infirmity" (Heb. 5:2). Every Christian worker should also have this compassion because he also is encompassed with infirmity. No one reaches perfection in this life. That is no reason to avoid serving others. Every believer may seek God's grace to enable him to be a blessing to others. Remembering the compassion of the Lord Jesus should stir up believers to manifest compassion to others. The Lord Jesus wept at the grave of Lazarus, sharing the sorrow of Mary and Martha (John 11:35). Believers today should have compassion.

PRAYER

Dear Lord, help us to be compassionate toward others. Give us a heart for the sorrows and trials of others. For Jesus' sake. Amen.

MAY 21

"**R**ighteous art thou, O Lord, when I plead with thee: yet let me talk with thee of thy judgments: wherefore doth the way of the wicked prosper? wherefore are all they happy that deal very treacherously?" (Jer. 12:1). The prophet knew that God was infinitely righteous, yet he was troubled over the question of why the wicked proper. But God is never in a hurry. He can bring the wicked to judgment, but He will do so in His own good time. Now He sends his rain on the just and the unjust, but the day will come when He brings judgment on the wicked. God promises blessing on the righteous, but it does not all come in this life. All the pleasure that the wicked experience, they get in this life only; the judgment is eternal. For God's people, all their pain is in this life only; their joy is eternal.

PRAYER

Dear Lord, help us to remember that our pain is in this life only; our joy in Your presence is eternal. For Jesus' sake. Amen.

MAY 22

"**B**ut if ye be led of the Spirit, ye are not under the law" (Gal. 5:18). Believers today do not just keep the Old Testament law; they submit to the leading of the indwelling Holy Spirit of God. He never leads contrary to the revealed Word of God. He leads away from fleshly sins to submission to the will of God. "But the fruit of the Spirit is love, joy, peace, longsuffering, gentleness, goodness, faith, meekness, temperance: against such there is no law" (Gal. 5:22–23). The Holy Spirit grows within the believer the likeness of Christ. He imparts to the believer the desire to be like Christ and to obey His Word. This is not legalism but freedom in Christ.

PRAYER

Dear Lord, lead us through Your Spirit that we may be like Christ, pleasing in Your sight. For Jesus' sake. Amen.

MAY 23

The Lord warned the Israelites, "If ye will not be reformed by me by these things, but will walk contrary unto me; then will I also walk contrary unto you, and will punish you yet seven times for your sins" (Lev. 26:23–24). Sin always has serious consequences. Foolish people think they can get away with sin, but there is a God in heaven Who is keeping track of all that is going on among the affairs of men. God brings judgment upon sin so that the sinner will forsake his sin and obey the Word of God. But God assures His people that if they will keep His commandments, He will walk among them and be their God (Lev. 26:3, 12). Every believer should purpose in his heart to walk humbly with God.

PRAYER

Dear Lord, forgive our waywardness; give us grace to walk with You in humble obedience. For Jesus' sake. Amen.

MAY 24

"**F**or to me to live is Christ, and to die is gain" (Phil. 1:21). The apostle Paul wrote from prison, expressing his devotion to the Lord Jesus Christ. If Paul was wrongfully executed, he was sure that he would go into the presence of the Lord he served. If he was released, he was determined to continue serving Christ with all his heart. Every Christian should remember Paul's example of trust. As long as we are in this world, we have the privilege of serving Christ and being a testimony for him. If we should die, there is no fear for the believer. He trusts in the keeping power of Christ. Paul wrote, "Therefore we are always confident, knowing that, whilst we are at home in the body, we are absent from the Lord . . . we are . . . willing rather to be absent from the body, and to be present with the Lord" (2 Cor. 5:6, 8).

PRAYER

Dear Lord, thank You for the privilege of serving You in this world, and when the right time comes, of serving You in heaven. Praise God!

MAY 25

"**W**hen a man's ways please the Lord, he maketh even his enemies to be at peace with him" (Prov. 16:7). The Lord knows when a person truly intends to please God. God can overrule and silence his enemies. "A man's heart deviseth his way: but the Lord directeth his steps" (Prov. 16:9). A man may plan his path carefully, but chance circumstances may completely foil his plans. God rules providentially in the life of every man. A wise man orders his life in the light of God's Word. No wonder Solomon exclaimed, "How much better is it to get wisdom than gold! and to get understanding rather to be chosen than silver! The highway of the upright is to depart from evil: he that keepeth his way preserveth his soul" (Prov. 16:16–17).

PRAYER

Dear Lord, give us the wisdom to avoid the evil and to choose the good. Give us a discerning spirit. For Jesus' sake. Amen.

MAY 26

The apostle Paul confessed, "And I persecuted this way unto the death, binding and delivering into prisons both men and women" (Acts 22:4). But Paul was now converted and was proclaiming the way of Christ before a multitude of his own countrymen. He now would face persecution and imprisonment for the sake of Christ. He was committed to the way of Christ because he had met the Lord Jesus on the Damascus road (Acts 9:1–7). We, too, need to be turned about into the way of Christ that His blood may blot out our sins and we may walk in His pathway to the glory of God. The Lord Jesus Christ is the beginning and the end of our pathway.

PRAYER

Dear Lord, give us clear direction in our life. Help us to walk Your pathway and be quick to tell others about You. Amen.

MAY 27

"O send out thy light and thy truth: let them lead me; let them bring me unto thy holy hill, and to thy tabernacles" (Ps. 43:3). The psalmist prayed that God's truth would lead him to God's presence. This is a noble prayer that all believers can echo. He called God "my exceeding joy" (v. 4*b*). Every believer should rejoice to think of the gracious presence of God that is with His people at all times. We should all be devouring God's truth, His holy Word, so that it may bring us closer to God. The more believers read and study God's Word, the more they understand about God's will and His leading in their lives. The Bible is God's light upon our pathway to guide us to Him.

PRAYER

Dear Lord, let the light of Your Word shine upon our hearts that it may guide us to You and Your path of blessing for our lives. For Jesus' sake. Amen.

MAY 28

Jesus said, "Yet a little while is the light with you. Walk while ye have the light, lest darkness come upon you; for he that walketh in darkness knoweth not whither he goeth" (John 12:35). Our faith should be in the Lord Jesus Christ, the light of the world. We should walk, that is, live our lives, in the light of His presence. The wicked world is a very dark place without His light. Sin and corruption surround us, but He illumines our pathway. The psalmist prayed, "Wilt not thou deliver my feet from falling, that I may walk before God in the light of the living?" (Ps. 56:13). He also solemnly vows, "I will walk before the Lord in the land of the living" (Ps. 116:9).

PRAYER

Dear Lord, help us to walk in the light of Your presence.
Illuminate our pathway by Your grace. For Jesus' sake. Amen.

MAY 29

"**H**e that walketh uprightly walketh surely: but he that perverteth his ways shall be known" (Prov. 10:9). The path that is upright in the eyes of God is a safe path. But the man who will walk a twisted path is soon known for his twisted life. The man who lives his life in the sight of God has a good conscience and peace of mind. But the devious man who tries to walk a dangerous pathway is soon recognized as undependable and dangerous. Every believer should live his life in the path that he knows to be the will of God. God will vindicate him and bless him. The Lord promises, "But to this man will I look, even to him that is poor and of a contrite spirit, and trembleth at my word" (Isa. 66:2*b*).

PRAYER

Dear Lord, give us grace to walk our pathway in obedience to Your Word, trusting in Your sustaining grace for every step. For Jesus' sake. Amen.

MAY 30

"**O**r despisest thou the riches of his goodness and forbearance and longsuffering; not knowing that the goodness of God leadeth thee to repentance?" (Rom. 2:4). People do not realize that God is gently leading them to repentance, to change for the better. People need to turn away from their sin and selfishness and turn to God, Who mercifully forgives and restores. God desires the best for His people, but that means turning away from what is wrong and sinful and turning to Him. "For there is no respect of persons with God" (Rom. 2:11). He cannot be impressed by self-righteousness, but He has compassion on the repentant. "Therefore being justified by faith, we have peace with God through our Lord Jesus Christ" (Rom. 5:1).

PRAYER

Dear God, forgive me my sin and failure through the merits of the Lord Jesus Christ. Restore the joy of my salvation. For Jesus' sake. Amen.

MAY 31

"**H**e leadeth me beside the still waters. He restoreth my soul: he leadeth me in the paths of righteousness for his name's sake" (Ps. 23:2*b*–3). The Lord Jesus Christ is our shepherd. He always leads His people on a safe path to His prepared home for them. Still waters are safe for the sheep to drink. Paths of righteousness are safe paths for His people to walk. The people of the world may rush heedlessly on dangerous pathways, but there are always consequences. The people who follow the good shepherd discover that goodness and mercy follow them all the days of their lives (v. 6). The home He is preparing for them is vastly better than anything they could imagine.

PRAYER

Dear Lord, give us grace to follow Your leading and to walk the pathway You have prepared for us. For Jesus' sake. Amen.

JUNE 1

"**T**he way of a fool is right in his own eyes; but he that hearkeneth unto counsel is wise" (Prov. 12:15). The person who thinks that his opinion is always right is only fooling himself. Seeking good advice is wise. But the best counsel is found in the Bible. The psalmist writes, "The entrance of thy words giveth light; it giveth understanding unto the simple" (Ps. 119:130). No wonder the psalmist exclaims, "O how love I thy law! it is my meditation all the day" (Ps. 119:97). "Thy testimonies have I taken as an heritage for ever: for they are the rejoicing of my heart" (Ps. 119:111). "Therefore I love thy commandments above gold; yea, above fine gold" (Ps. 119:127).

PRAYER

Dear Lord, guide us into paths of wisdom through Your Word. Help us to see the right path to please You. For Jesus' sake. Amen.

JUNE 2

"**Y**ea, they are greedy dogs which can never have enough, and they are shepherds that cannot understand: they all look to their own way, every one for his gain, from his quarter" (Isa. 56:11). The prophet denounces the greed and injustice in the land. People look to their own way, seeking gain, rather than obeying the Word of the Lord. The watchmen who ought to warn the people are like dumb dogs that cannot bark (v. 10). The moral situation sounds like our own day. "The righteous perisheth, and no man layeth it to heart" (Isa. 57:1). We need to seek the way of the Lord and to speak out against what we know to be wrong. Judgment is coming to our own generation.

PRAYER

O Lord, have mercy on our sinful generation. Help us to turn away from sin and to walk Your pathway. For Jesus' sake. Amen.

JUNE 3

"**F**or we walk by faith, not by sight" (2 Cor. 5:7). The believer cannot see the celestial realm in which God's throne rules over all. Yet he walks by faith, seeking to do the things that please his heavenly Father. People may sneer at his religious devotion, but the faithful believer will persevere in obedience to God's holy Word. We may be troubled on every side, but we do not despair (2 Cor. 4:8). The believer always remembers the clear revelation, "For we must all appear before the judgment seat of Christ; that every one may receive the things done in his body, according to that he hath done, whether it be good or bad" (2 Cor. 5:10).

PRAYER

Dear Lord, help us to walk our path faithfully, always remembering that we are walking homeward to You. For Jesus' sake. Amen.

JUNE 4

"**A**nd I will bring the blind by a way that they knew not; I will lead them in paths that they have not known: I will make darkness light before them, and crooked things straight. These things will I do unto them, and not forsake them" (Isa. 42:16). Thus the Lord warns His ancient people. He will make their sinful path difficult, but He will not forsake them. The Lord often brings chastisement into the lives of His people, but He does not forsake them. He declares, "I am the Lord: that is my name: and my glory will I not give to another, neither my praise to graven images" (Isa. 42:8). God's people need to forsake their idols and turn back to the living God, Who can deliver them.

PRAYER

Dear Lord, have mercy on Your sinful people. Turn us back to You and lead us in paths only You can find. For Jesus' sake. Amen.

JUNE 5

"**A**s ye have therefore received Christ Jesus the Lord, so walk ye in him: rooted and built up in him, and stablished in the faith, as ye have been taught, abounding therein with thanksgiving" (Col. 2:6–7). To walk in Christ is to live the life in submission to His will. All believers need to be established in the faith with deep roots in the teaching of the Lord Jesus Christ. Our daily lives should manifest the depth of our devotion to Him. All believers should be abounding with thanksgiving over all the multitude of blessings that the Lord Jesus has brought into our lives. We live our lives in Him, in His grace, in His strength, in His love.

PRAYER

Thank You, Lord Jesus, for all the blessings and grace that You pour out upon us. Help us to keep on walking in Your grace and strength. Amen.

JUNE 6

God's ancient people had plunged into gross sin, but they were saying "the Lord seeth not" (Ezek. 9:9*b*). But the Lord's response was "I will recompense their way upon their head" (Ezek. 9:10*b*). Scripture assures us in the creation account, "God saw every thing that he had made" (Gen. 1:31*a*). He still does. People need to live their lives with the thought that God is indeed observing everything that is being done. Believers should make sure that their way is pleasing to the Lord. Day by day they need to walk with God in humble obedience. Unbelievers need to forsake their wicked way and turn to God for forgiveness and cleansing. He is ready to forgive and cleanse their way.

PRAYER

Dear Lord, forgive us our sins and cleanse us from them. Help us to walk Your way in humble obedience. For Jesus' sake. Amen.

JUNE 7

"We exhorted and comforted and charged every one of you . . . that ye would walk worthy of God, who hath called you unto his kingdom and glory" (1 Thess. 2:11–12). The apostle Paul fervently exhorts all believers to walk, that is, live their lives, in a manner worthy of God. God summons believers to His kingdom and the glory of heaven. We should live as pilgrims, traveling through this world on a pathway that leads to heaven. We must not put down deep roots here. This world is not our home; God has prepared something far better for us in that celestial city of God (Rev. 21:9–27). In this world we should live as God's people, desiring to please Him above all things.

PRAYER

Dear Lord, quicken our steps toward Your heavenly home for us. Guide us and protect us on our pilgrim pathway. For Jesus' sake. Amen.

JUNE 8

"All the paths of the Lord are mercy and truth unto such as keep his covenant and his testimonies" (Ps. 25:10). Obedience to God's Word always brings blessing into the lives of His people. Whatever path the Lord may call us to walk, we are blessed when we walk in step with His Word. David could say, "Mine eyes are ever toward the Lord; for he shall pluck my feet out of the net" (Ps. 25:15). People may spread nets to catch us, but the Lord is able to deliver us out of the snare. Walking the Lord's pathway always leads homeward. We must continue to walk with God along life's pathway, for He always blesses those who keep His Word.

PRAYER

Dear Lord, help us to walk Your pathway in the light of Your Word. Guide our steps by Your Word. For Jesus' sake. Amen.

JUNE 9

"**W**oe unto them! for they have gone in the way of Cain, and ran greedily after the error of Balaam for reward, and perished in the gainsaying of Core" (Jude 11). Jude solemnly warns against the apostate teachers of his day. In our own day there are false teachers who deny the truth of the Bible and lead people astray. Jude goes on to refer to these false teachers "to whom is reserved the blackness of darkness for ever" (Jude 13). God will judge false teachers. But God will also reveal the truth of His Word to those who genuinely seek Him. Jude also exhorts, "But ye, beloved . . . keep yourselves in the love of God, looking for the mercy of our Lord Jesus Christ unto eternal life" (Jude 20–21).

PRAYER

Dear God, preserve us from the false teachers of our own day and lead us by Your Word into pathways of blessing and service for You. For Jesus' sake. Amen.

JUNE 10

"**H**e that walketh with wise men shall be wise: but a companion of fools shall be destroyed" (Prov. 13:20). The association with those who are wise brings positive benefits from their example and counsel. It is always easier to choose wisely when those around are making wise choices. On the other hand it is easy for someone to make disastrous mistakes when those around them are doing the same thing. The choice of companions affects the whole direction of life. It is vital that the believer walk with God and with those whose direction in life is toward the things of God. "He that diligently seeketh good procureth favour: but he that seeketh mischief, it shall come unto him" (Prov. 11:27).

PRAYER

O Lord, give us the wisdom to walk with You and to turn our backs on those who live like fools. For Jesus' sake. Amen.

June 11

"Let us walk honestly, as in the day; not in rioting and drunkenness, not in chambering and wantonness, not in strife and envying" (Rom. 13:13). The apostle exhorts believers to live their lives honestly, as in broad daylight, honoring the Lord in their conduct. The sins of drunkenness, violence, and sexual sins should not be found among believers. Those who claim the Lord Jesus as their Savior have the responsibility to be good testimonies for Him in this wicked world. The secret of having a good testimony is the presence of the Lord Jesus Himself with the believer. "But put ye on the Lord Jesus Christ, and make not provision for the flesh, to fulfil the lusts thereof" (Rom. 13:14). His presence is a robe of protection.

Prayer

Lord Jesus, help us to live for You each day. Give us a sense of Your presence with us day by day. Amen.

JUNE 12

"**D**an shall be a serpent by the way, an adder in the path, that biteth the horse heels, so that his rider shall fall backward" (Gen. 49:17). This is a solemn warning that some people are very dangerous to meet. They are like a poisonous snake on the path, ready to strike. Believers should take pains to avoid them. Jacob had seen enough of them in his life. Now he was saying, "I have waited for thy salvation, O Lord" (Gen. 49:18). God's pathway is always best. The path of wicked people may look exciting and even profitable, but it always leads to disaster. God's Word warns, "Be sure your sin will find you out" (Num. 32:23). Jesus invites, "Come unto me, all ye that labour and are heavy laden, and I will give you rest" (Matt. 11:28).

PRAYER

Dear Lord, guide our steps away from the dangers of our day and lead us to Yourself by Your grace. Amen.

JUNE 13

"He that saith he abideth in him ought himself also so to walk, even as he walked" (1 John 2:6). The person who claims to know the Lord Jesus Christ as Savior and Lord ought to be living a life that reflects that faith and obedience. John, the apostle of love, says very sharply, "He that saith, I know him, and keepeth not his commandments, is a liar, and the truth is not in him" (1 John 2:4). But he goes on to say, "But whoso keepeth his word, in him verily is the love of God perfected: hereby know we that we are in him" (1 John 2:5). The walk of every believer should send a message of faithful trust and obedience in the Lord Jesus Christ. "But whoso keepeth his word, in him verily is the love of God perfected" (1 John 2:5).

PRAYER

Dear Lord Jesus, help us to live our lives for You. Give us grace to show Your love and compassion to all we meet. In Your name. Amen.

JUNE 14

The prophet warns his people against the sins of Samaria and Sodom and goes on to say, "Yet hast thou not walked after their ways, nor done after their abominations: but, as if that were a very little thing, thou wast corrupted more than they in all thy ways" (Ezek. 16:47). Yet God deals graciously with sinners. He goes on to say, "Nevertheless I will remember my covenant with thee in the days of thy youth, and I will establish unto thee an everlasting covenant. Then thou shalt remember thy ways, and be ashamed" (Ezek. 16:60–61*a*). God is ready to forgive the repentant sinner and to restore the blessings of salvation to those who seek His face.

PRAYER

Lord Jesus, forgive our sins and restore to us the joy of our salvation that we may walk with You in paths of righteousness. Amen.

June 15

"**A**nd make straight paths for your feet, lest that which is lame be turned out of the way; but let it rather be healed" (Heb. 12:13). There are times when the believer stumbles along the pathway. That is not a time for self-pity but rather for correction and renewed progress. "Wherefore lift up the hands which hang down, and the feeble knees" (v. 12). It is a time for renewed grace and strength from the Lord. We must go forward in straight paths on the way of blessing that God leads us. "Follow peace with all men, and holiness, without which no man shall see the Lord" (Heb. 12:14). God always leads His people on paths of righteousness and blessing.

PRAYER

O Lord, strengthen us for the pathway and give us grace to walk with You, expecting blessing and sustaining grace. For Jesus' sake. Amen.

JUNE 16

"**T**he hoary head is a crown of glory, if it be found in the way of righteousness" (Prov. 16:31). The person who has white hair is a demonstration of having survived the trials and tests of life. But if that person is also a strong believer, he is a testimony for the sustaining grace and care of almighty God. Walking in the way of righteousness implies living the life to the glory of God. It means being a witness for God by word and deed in the daily round of life. The world is watching; therefore, the believer must be careful to maintain a clear testimony for Christ. The mature believer can remember the many blessings that God has provided in the past; he is sure that God will never fail him.

PRAYER

Dear God, help us to live for You and to be a testimony for Your sustaining grace through all of life. For Jesus' sake. Amen.

June 17

"**B**ut as God hath distributed to every man, as the Lord hath called every one, so let him walk. And so ordain I in all churches" (1 Cor. 7:17). The apostle Paul encouraged believers to be content with the circumstances in which the Lord placed them. We are where we are because God put us there to be a testimony for Him. In the midst of trials the Lord can impart to us His sustaining grace. People need to see that God's grace is sufficient for whatever circumstances may arise. God has promised, "I will never leave thee, nor forsake thee" (Heb. 13:5). The biblical writer adds, "So that we may boldly say, The Lord is my helper, and I will not fear what man shall do unto me" (Heb. 13:6).

PRAYER

Dear Lord, help us to remember that You are always with us, to sustain us and guide us on our pilgrim pathway. For Jesus' sake. Amen.

JUNE 18

"**B**e not wise in thine own eyes: fear the Lord, and depart from evil" (Prov. 3:7). Too many people think that they can get away with sin, but God is watching. The believer must reverence God and turn away from what he knows is evil. He must allow God to direct his paths (v. 6). That always means to leave what he knows is wrong and instead to walk in pathways that please God. God always leads the believer into paths of reverence and service. "For whom the Lord loveth he correcteth; even as a father the son in whom he delighteth" (Prov. 3:12). The believer needs a teachable spirit that will heed the instruction of the Lord and humbly walk His pathway.

PRAYER

Dear Lord, help me to walk with You in paths of service and blessing. Enable me to be a blessing to others. For Jesus' sake. Amen.

June 19

"**F**urthermore then we beseech you, brethren, and exhort you by the Lord Jesus, that as ye have received of us how ye ought to walk and to please God, so ye would abound more and more" (1 Thess. 4:1). Believers ought to grow in grace and in the knowledge of the Lord Jesus Christ. Paul here exhorts believers to take his teaching concerning the Lord Jesus and to make progress in living out the teaching they have received. The Christian life must not be just theory; it must be the living practice of all true believers. People ought to be able to recognize Christians by the way they live. True believers practice the teaching of the Lord Jesus in their daily lives.

Prayer

Dear Lord, give us grace to live for You. Grant that our lives may demonstrate our love for You. Amen.

JUNE 20

"Remove from me the way of lying: and grant me thy law graciously" (Ps. 119:29). The psalmist prays that God remove the worldly ways of lying from him and instead give him graciously the truth of God. Believers need to consciously turn away from sinful practices and seek the grace of God instead. The psalmist goes on to say, "I have chosen the way of truth: thy judgments have I laid before me" (Ps. 119:30). The believer must deliberately choose to obey God's will. The psalmist opens the Word of God to fill his mind with the strength of Scripture in order that he might walk in a way that pleases God. All believers need to follow his example in filling their minds with Scripture.

PRAYER

Dear Lord, enable me to fill my mind with your holy Word that its strength may empower me to walk with You. For Jesus' sake. Amen.

JUNE 21

"The Holy Ghost this signifying, that the way into the holiest of all was not yet made manifest, while as the first tabernacle was yet standing" (Heb. 9:8). The Old Testament believer was not allowed into the most holy place. The gifts and sacrifices offered then could not make the believer perfect (v. 9). But the coming of Christ changed everything. "How much more shall the blood of Christ, who through the eternal Spirit offered himself without spot to God, purge your conscience from dead works to serve the living God?" (Heb. 9:14). The Lord Jesus Christ said, "I am the way, the truth, and the life: no man cometh unto the Father, but by me" (John 14:6).

PRAYER

Thank You, Lord Jesus, for sacrificing Yourself for our sins that we might come to God through You. Open our eyes to Your truth. Amen.

JUNE 22

"**U**nderstanding shall keep thee: to deliver thee from the way of the evil man, from the man that speaketh froward things; who leave the paths of uprightness, to walk in the ways of darkness" (Prov. 2:11–13). It is the part of wisdom to turn away from those who draw you toward evil practices. If people walk in ways of darkness, turn away from them and walk instead in the light of the Word of God. God shines His blessed light upon those who walk in His ways. The believer who walks the path of uprightness will find fellowship with God and with His saints along the way. That is the path that leads to home with God and His people.

PRAYER

Dear Lord, give us grace to walk with You in the light. Lead us to Yourself and the eternal home You have prepared. For Jesus' sake. Amen.

JUNE 23

"Walk in wisdom toward them that are without, redeeming the time" (Col. 4:5). The believer must be careful to maintain a good testimony toward those who are unbelievers. Their speech ought to be always "with grace, seasoned with salt" (Col. 4:6). Unbelievers are always watching believers to see if their walk, their practice, matches their testimony. Believers ought to "buy up" the opportunity to be a witness to them. Paul asked believers to pray for him that God would open a "door of utterance" for him (Col. 4:3). Believers today ought to ask God for such a "door of utterance."

PRAYER

Dear Lord, help us to live for You and to be a testimony for Your grace and love to those about us. For Jesus' sake. Amen.

JUNE 24

"**T**hy way, O God, is in the sanctuary: who is so great a God as our God?" (Ps. 77:13). The psalmist had learned to worship God and to meet Him in the sanctuary. He knew him as the one true God, vastly above the idols of men, the God Who can work wonders for His people (v. 14). So he vows to meditate on the works of God (v. 12). All believers need to meditate on the greatness of God and ponder His loving deeds in behalf of His people. We, too, need to tell others of the greatness of our God. The sense of His presence with us is a benediction all the day.

PRAYER

Thank You, Lord, for Your loving care and protection. Help us to walk in fellowship with You all the day. For Jesus' sake. Amen.

JUNE 25

"**F**or they themselves shew of us what manner of entering in we had unto you, and how ye turned to God from idols to serve the living and true God" (1 Thess. 1:9). The apostle Paul made a powerful impression on the Thessalonians. He preached the gospel to them and they turned away from their idols to serve the one true God. This is a standing reminder to all believers that they must turn from the idols of the past and devote themselves to the service of the one true God, the Lord of the universe. He is the blessed Trinity, Father, Son, and Holy Spirit. It was the Son, the Lord Jesus Christ, Who delivered us from the wrath to come.

PRAYER

Dear Lord, help us to so live that people may recognize that we have turned away from idols to serve You alone. For Jesus' sake. Amen.

JUNE 26

God warns, "For mine eyes are upon all their ways: they are not hid from my face, neither is their iniquity hid from mine eyes" (Jer. 16:17). He is speaking about the sins of His people, who think they can hide their sins from God. But no one can hide his sins from an omniscient God. Jeremiah responds by crying out to God, "O Lord, my strength, and my fortress, and my refuge in the day of affliction" (Jer. 16:19*a*). The only way to deal with sin is to turn to God, Who can forgive it and restore the person. We, too, must walk humbly with God, Who sees our sins and can remove them by the blood of Christ our Savior.

PRAYER

Dear Lord, blot out our sins by the merits of the Lord Jesus Christ and restore us to fellowship with You for His sake. Amen.

JUNE 27

The apostle Paul declared before the governor Felix, "But this I confess unto thee, that after the way which they call heresy, so worship I the God of my fathers, believing all things which are written in the law and the prophets" (Acts 24:14). Others may look down on the "way" of Christianity, but Paul was committed to that way. He knew the Lord Jesus as his Savior and was determined to spread the gospel to all he could reach. We, too, must be bold in our faith in the Lord Jesus. We must not be intimidated by the opposition of the world. It has always cost something to be a faithful follower of the Lord Jesus. Today it is our turn to stand boldly to confess that we are Christians, followers of the Lord Jesus Christ.

PRAYER

Dear Lord, give us faith and courage to speak for You in the midst of a wicked generation. For Jesus' sake. Amen.

JUNE 28

"**B**lessed is the people that know the joyful sound: they shall walk, O Lord, in the light of thy countenance" (Ps. 89:15). The psalmist sings of the mercy and faithfulness of God: "I will sing of the mercies of the Lord for ever: with my mouth will I make known thy faithfulness to all generations" (Ps. 89:1). People who understand the nature of God will walk in humble obedience to His Word. They can say, "For the Lord is our defence" (Ps. 89:18). The protection of the Lord's presence brings joy and singing to God's people. It is our part to walk in humble obedience to His Word. The psalmist sang, "In thy name shall they rejoice all the day" (Ps. 89:16).

PRAYER

Dear Lord, help us to walk in Your presence with joyful obedience to Your holy Word. For Jesus' sake. Amen.

JUNE 29

"Then they cried unto the Lord in their trouble. . . . And he led them forth by the right way, that they might go to a city of habitation" (Ps. 107:6–7). Whenever God's people turn to Him and cry out for His help, God leads His people into the right path of blessing. It is always harmful for God's people to struggle along without asking for His guidance. God has a will for His people and can guide them. But they must seek His guidance and walk humbly in His pathway. Walking with God should be the believer's highest goal. To keep in step with God's plan means His highest blessing can rest upon us.

PRAYER

Dear Lord, give us grace to walk with You along the path of Your will for our lives. For Jesus' sake. Amen.

JUNE 30

The Pharisees and the Herodians plotted together to trick the Lord Jesus by asking, "Master, we know that thou art true, and teachest the way of God in truth. . . . Tell us therefore. . . Is it lawful to give tribute unto Caesar, or not?" (Matt. 22:17*b*). Whichever way He answered, one group was ready to pounce on His answer. But He gave a perfect answer: Worship God and pay your taxes (v. 21). The believer must learn to meet all his responsibilities. The believer should be an honest citizen and a devout worshiper of God at the same time. The believer's life should not reflect revolution but devotion to God and to others.

PRAYER

Dear Lord, help us to be good citizens but to put You first in our hearts. For Jesus' sake. Amen.

JULY 1

"**M**y son, forget not my law; but let thine heart keep my commandments: for length of days, and long life, and peace, shall they add to thee" (Prov. 3:1–2). God's Word always adds blessing to the life of every believer. It creates serenity in the face of hardship, peace in times of stress, and joy in the face of sorrow. Every believer must steep his soul in the truths of God's Word. The Bible is a life-transforming book. We need to meditate upon it and let its truths transform our lives so that we become faithful servants and good witnesses for the Lord. The Bible is the most valuable possession that any believer can have. We should seek to wear it out by our daily use.

PRAYER

Thank You, Lord, for the precious gift of Your holy Word. Fill our hearts with its truths and help us to live what we learn. For Jesus' sake. Amen.

JULY 2

"**I**n his favour is life: weeping may endure for a night, but joy cometh in the morning" (Ps. 30:5*b*). The good favor of God makes life worth living. Sorrow and disappointment may come in the night, but with the morning light comes the reassurance of the presence of God and His sustaining grace. Trials of life may come, but God never forsakes His people. There is always a new day and renewed opportunity to see the hand of God leading and blessing His people. The psalmist cried to the Lord for mercy (v. 10) and then declared, "Thou hast turned for me my mourning into dancing: thou hast put off my sackcloth, and girded me with gladness" (v. 11).

PRAYER

Dear Lord, help me to see Your hand of guidance and lead me into paths of blessing in Your presence. For Jesus' sake. Amen.

JULY 3

"**E**very way of a man is right in his own eyes: but the Lord pondereth the hearts" (Prov. 21:2). It is human nature for people to assume they are in the right and others are wrong. But the Lord God carefully examines the heart of every individual. He knows when a person acts out of selfish unconcern for others. Solomon warned, "An high look, and a proud heart, and the plowing of the wicked, is sin" (Prov. 21:4). Something as neutral as plowing a field can be sin if the person's heart is not right with God. God sees the heart, and hence it is very important for every person to get his own heart right with God.

PRAYER

Dear Lord, cleanse my heart from selfishness. Help me to think of others and to be a blessing to those in need. For Jesus' sake. Amen.

JULY 4

"**F**or so is the will of God, that with well doing ye may put to silence the ignorance of foolish men: as free, and not using your liberty for a cloke of maliciousness, but as the servants of God" (1 Pet. 2:15–16). The believer should maintain a walk of well doing. He is free, but not free to do whatever he wants. He is set free from sin so that he may serve God by walking in a pathway that honors God and blesses his neighbor. The path of well doing is a testimony to all that he has put God first in his life and intends to continue living for God in his daily walk. Peter may well ask, "And who is he that will harm you, if ye be followers of that which is good?" (1 Pet. 3:13).

PRAYER

Dear Lord, help us to live as those who are set free from sin and are now devoted to living for Christ in this present world. For Jesus' sake. Amen.

JULY 5

"**B**lessed is every one that feareth the Lord; that walketh in his ways" (Ps. 128:1). Reverence for God is a great blessing to believers. To walk with God is to live the life in the consciousness of His presence. In the hurry and bustle of today's world the believer can have an internal peace that comes from the knowledge of the presence of God with him. God guides his steps and gives him the assurance of His protecting hand in all of life's busy round. Reverence for God preserves him from going with the wrong people down the dangerous pathway that leads away from God. God's presence is a fortress of protection.

PRAYER

Thank You, Lord, for inviting me to walk with You through the pathways of life. Help me to walk with You and talk with You along the way. For Jesus' sake. Amen.

JULY 6

"**Y**ea, and all that will live godly in Christ Jesus shall suffer persecution" (2 Tim. 3:12). A good testimony for Christ attracts the opposition of the Devil and wicked men, but their attacks cannot harm the believer. Paul mentioned the persecutions and afflictions that came to him, "but out of them all the Lord delivered me" (v. 11). And thus God watches over His servants. God gave His inspired Scriptures to His people to instruct them in righteousness (2 Tim. 3:16). Continued obedience to His Word always leads to blessing from God. That is a testimony that every believer needs to maintain. God will continue blessing His people.

PRAYER

O Lord, help us to live as good testimonies for You. Give us grace to please You above all. For Jesus' sake. Amen.

JULY 7

"**I** the Lord search the heart, I try the reins, even to give to every man according to his ways, and according to the fruit of his doings" (Jer. 17:10). The Lord God declares that He sees the heart of every man. He will repay every person according to his doings. Those who sin with a high hand will find judgment waiting for them, but those who walk humbly with God will find mercy and grace waiting for them. Jeremiah was speaking to His rebellious people, but every man will find that his words are true. The nature of God does not change. Every man who seeks the face of God in contrition will find it, and every one who goes on in his sin will find judgment waiting for him at the end.

PRAYER

Dear Lord, forgive us our willful deeds and by Your grace turn us about to paths of righteousness. For Jesus' sake. Amen.

JULY 8

"**T**hou leddest thy people like a flock by the hand of Moses and Aaron" (Ps. 77:20). The leaders of Israel were simply instruments in the hand of God to deliver His people. To this day all pastors and leaders of the church are simply instruments in the hand of God to lead and bless His people. They can take no credit, for it is God's power that leads and guides His earthly people. But that is a good reason for people to pray for their leaders that they may lead them according to God's will in paths of blessing and service. Did not the apostle Paul write: "Brethren, pray for us, that the word of the Lord may have free course, and be glorified, even as it is with you" (2 Thess. 3:1)?

PRAYER

Dear Lord, bless and guide our pastors and leaders that they may direct our steps into paths of service and blessing. For Jesus' sake. Amen.

JULY 9

"**O** the depth of the riches both of the wisdom and knowledge of God! how unsearchable are his judgments, and his ways past finding out!" (Rom. 11:33). Reverence for God, "The fear of the Lord is the beginning of wisdom" (Ps. 111:10). The Spirit of the Lord is called "the spirit of wisdom and understanding" (Isa. 11:2). Every believer needs the wisdom of God to direct his paths. "If any of you lack wisdom, let him ask of God, that giveth to all men liberally, and upbraideth not; and it shall be given him" (James 1:5). How great is the kindness of God to impart His wisdom to His people! Let us ask Him for His wisdom that we may live for Him in this world.

PRAYER

Dear Lord, by Your grace impart to us Your wisdom that we may live for You with a good testimony in this world. For Jesus' sake. Amen.

JULY 10

"**Y**e say, The way of the Lord is not equal. Hear now, O house of Israel; Is not my way equal? are not your ways unequal? When a righteous man turneth away from his righteousness, and committeth iniquity . . . for his iniquity that he hath done shall he die. Again, when the wicked man turneth away from his wickedness that he hath committed, and doeth that which is lawful and right, he shall save his soul alive" (Ezek. 18:25–27). The Lord always judges fairly and accurately. We are the ones who come short and stand condemned by our deeds. We all need the grace of the Lord's forgiveness and cleansing. The Lord Jesus Christ was the One Who was "wounded for our transgressions" (Isa. 53:5*a*). He alone saves.

PRAYER

Thank You, Lord Jesus, for dying for my sins. Cleanse me from them and help me to live for You from now on. Amen.

JULY 11

"**F**or with thee is the fountain of life: in thy light shall we see light" (Ps. 36:9). The Lord provides life and light for His people. He is the originator and source of both. His people need to keep coming to Him for both their life and light. The absence of God means death and darkness. Believers search the Scriptures to learn of His glorious light. They continue searching the Scriptures to learn of that eternal life that is found in the Lord Jesus Christ alone. The Lord Jesus said, "I am the light of the world: he that followeth me shall not walk in darkness, but shall have the light of life" (John 8:12). Believers need to turn their eyes to Jesus and walk in His light.

PRAYER

Dear Lord, help us to see Your light and to walk with You in the light of Your presence. Amen.

JULY 12

"**T**rain up a child in the way he should go: and when he is old, he will not depart from it" (Prov. 22:6). He may be inconsistent when he is young, but when he matures, he will understand the need for principle and character. And he will have in his memory the training and consistent life of his parents. The training of the young is one of the great privileges of parents. Proper training can make the pathway much easier for the young. Reverence for God is one of the most important attitudes to instill in the young. For children to see Bible reading and prayer as a normal part of daily life is one of the most important things for them to learn.

PRAYER

Dear Lord, help us to so live for You that others may see the importance of consistent living in the midst of daily life. For Jesus' sake. Amen.

July 13

"**F**or the grace of God . . . hath appeared to all men, teaching us that, denying ungodliness and worldly lusts, we should live soberly, righteously, and godly, in this present world" (Titus 2:11–12). The believer in Christ should live his faith day by day in the face of the world's view. If the believer allows the world around him to silence his religious beliefs, he is a poor witness for Christ. But the best witness for Christ is not mere talk; it is that sober, consistent life of good works and kindness to those about him. This present world, with all its sin and wickedness, is the scene in which the believer is to live out his faith in the Lord Jesus Christ.

Prayer

Dear Lord, help me to so live that all who know me will recognize that I live for the Lord Jesus and His testimony. For Jesus' sake. Amen.

JULY 14

"**H**ear my cry, O God; attend unto my prayer. From the end of the earth will I cry unto thee, when my heart is overwhelmed: lead me to the rock that is higher than I" (Ps. 61:1–2). The wise thing for believers is to turn to the Lord in times of distress. The psalmist could say, "For thou hast been a shelter for me, and a strong tower from the enemy" (v. 3). Every believer needs the protection of God's presence with him. We must not fall into self confidence. God alone is able to guide us safely through the tests and snares of this life. David put his trust in the Lord his God. His testimony was "So will I sing praise unto thy name for ever" (v. 8).

PRAYER

Dear Lord, help me to walk with You through the trials and tests of life. Preserve me from the snares and help me to keep in step. For Jesus' sake. Amen.

July 15

"**T**he fruit of the righteous is a tree of life; and he that winneth souls is wise" (Prov. 11:30). The way a righteous person lives bears fruit in the lives of those around him. They can see his life of devotion to God and know that it ought to be in their lives as well. The believer who makes the effort to win others to Christ is a testimony to all those about him. The wisdom of God rests upon him. God rewards those who live for Him. But in the opposite direction the Lord repays the wicked as well. "Behold, the righteous shall be recompensed in the earth: much more the wicked and the sinner" (Prov. 11:31).

PRAYER

Dear Lord, help us to live for You in this world. May our lives be a testimony for You in this wicked generation. For Jesus' sake. Amen.

JULY 16

"**B**ut covet earnestly the best gifts: and yet shew I unto you a more excellent way" (1 Cor. 12:31). The pathway of love is more excellent than all spiritual gifts. You can have the tongues of men and angels and without love be as sounding brass (1 Cor. 13:1). People are moved to God by acts of love and kindness far more than the most eloquent speech could ever do. Believers should seek to use the gifts that God has given them, but the love of Christ is still the most important thing in reaching out to the lost. Christ loves sinners and died for them that they might be saved. That is the truth that moves people to God.

PRAYER

Dear Lord, let Your love flow through us to reach others for You. Give us a heart of compassion for others. For Jesus' sake. Amen.

JULY 17

"**N**ow therefore thus saith the Lord of hosts; Consider your ways" (Hag. 1:5). It is a good thing for every person to stop to consider the way he is traveling. In the case of the Israelites, they were working hard and accomplishing nothing. They were putting their wages "into a bag with holes" (v. 6*b*). We, too, must consider whether we are wasting time and effort for nothing. Mere accumulation of worldly goods satisfies no one. That person always need "more." But the right relationship with God satisfies completely. If He is central in our lives, there will be complete satisfaction in the worship and service of the one true God. We must walk in the pathway He marks out before us to find true satisfaction.

PRAYER

Dear Lord, give us guidance and wisdom in walking our pathway in Your sight. Help us to please You above all things. For Jesus' sake. Amen.

July 18

"**H**ear thou, my son, and be wise, and guide thine heart in the way" (Prov. 23:19). Solomon urged his son to listen to his advice and to guide his heart in the way of the Lord. He warned that "the drunkard and the glutton shall come to poverty" (v. 21). Instead he urged, "Buy the truth, and sell it not; also wisdom, and instruction, and understanding" (v. 23). The truth of God's Word is still a treasure that people should count very precious. Wisdom comes only from the all-wise God. We all need to search the Scriptures for the wisdom of God for our lives. "Through wisdom is an house builded; and by understanding it is established" (Prov. 24:3). The wisdom of God can build and establish our homes.

Prayer

Dear Lord, give us hearts that treasure Your Word; enable us to walk according to the teaching of Your Word. For Jesus' sake. Amen.

JULY 19

"**F**or we hear that there are some which walk among you disorderly, working not at all, but are busybodies" (2 Thess. 3:11). Paul had heard that some among the Thessalonians were not maintaining a proper Christian testimony. His words direct all believers to live a life that is unquestionably Christian. Believers are not to be lazy, or meddling in the affairs of others, but they should be living their lives for the Lord Jesus Christ. Paul delivers an apostolic command to believers: "Now them that are such we command and exhort by our Lord Jesus Christ, that with quietness they work, and eat their own bread" (2 Thess. 3:12). Believers should be a wholesome testimony of faithfulness to the Lord Jesus Christ to all who know them.

PRAYER

Dear Lord, help us to be a testimony of faithfulness to You in our regular way of living day by day for You. For Jesus' sake. Amen.

JULY 20

"**M**ine eyes shall be upon the faithful of the land, that they may dwell with me: he that walketh in a perfect way, he shall serve me" (Ps. 101:6). These words do not reflect merely the pious thought of David; they convey the eternal purpose of God Himself. David wrote elsewhere, "I have declared thy faithfulness and thy salvation" (Ps. 40:10). He celebrated the faithfulness of God, but God desires faithfulness in His people as well. David vowed, "I will set no wicked thing before mine eyes" (Ps. 101:3). He wished to center his attention upon God and His holy Word. That is a noble purpose for believers even to this day. We too need to walk with faithful believers along God's pathway.

PRAYER

Dear Lord, help us to walk with You along the pathway of Your will. Give us grace to be a help to others along the way. For Jesus' sake. Amen.

JULY 21

"**H**ear thou, my son, and be wise, and guide thine heart in the way" (Prov. 23:19). Solomon exhorted his son to listen to the words of the wise. "Buy the truth, and sell it not; also wisdom, and instruction, and understanding" (Prov. 23:23). Those who turn away from wise counsel shall run into disaster. The believer must walk humbly in the path of the Word of God. To turn aside is to perish. To walk according to the Word of God is to walk with God in the path that leads to eternal life. "Let not thine heart envy sinners: but be thou in the fear of the Lord all the day long" (Prov. 23:17). Reverence for God always leads to the right path.

PRAYER

Dear Lord, guide our steps according to Your Word. Enable us to walk with You homeward. For Jesus' sake. Amen.

JULY 22

The prophet Jeremiah proclaimed to his people a solemn message: "Thus saith the Lord . . . return ye now every one from his evil way, and make your ways and your doings good" (Jer. 18:11). But their response was "we will walk after our own devices" (Jer. 18:12). The Lord's judgment was "Because my people hath forgotten me . . . I will scatter them as with an east wind before the enemy" (Jer. 18:15, 17). When an individual, or a nation, turns away from God, there are always disastrous consequences. The Lord pronounced the judgment: "They shall bury them in Tophet, till there be no place to bury" (Jer. 19:11). Every generation must repent and turn to God or face solemn judgment.

PRAYER

O Lord, have mercy upon us and bring us back to You. Help us to walk humbly with You in the midst of a wicked generation. For Jesus' sake. Amen.

July 23

"**F**or as many as are led by the Spirit of God, they are the sons of God" (Rom. 8:14). The life of the believer is not an adventure into unknown territory. It is a life of submission to the leading of the Spirit of God. Just as an earthly father would not expect his young child to walk a dangerous path alone, so our heavenly Father leads His children by His indwelling Spirit. The Spirit of God illuminates Scripture in order to shed light upon the pathway of God's children. This is why reading the Bible is such an important thing for believers to do. If they do not read God's message to them, how can they know the right pathway to take?

Prayer

Dear Lord, illuminate Your Word to us that we may walk with You on the pathway of Your will for our lives. For Jesus' sake. Amen.

JULY 24

The Lord said to Moses concerning the Israelites, "They have turned aside quickly out of the way which I commanded them: they have made them a molten calf. . . . Now therefore let me alone, that my wrath may wax hot against them" (Exod. 32:8, 10). Moses understood that the Lord was not really forbidding Him to pray for his people but rather was provoking him to intercede for them. We, too, must not cease praying for the lost. They may look hopeless and act bitter, but we must still intercede for them that the Lord may have mercy upon them and bring them to Himself. We, too, were once lost and needed prayer.

PRAYER

Dear Lord, give us a burden to pray for the lost even though they may be ungrateful. For Jesus' sake. Amen.

JULY 25

"**Y**ea, the Lord shall give that which is good; and our land shall yield her increase. Righteousness shall go before him; and shall set us in the way of his steps" (Ps. 85:12–13). God delights in doing what is good. We need to pray that He will set us in the way of His steps. We tend to go astray, but His way is always best. By His grace He will give His people what is good: eternal life in His presence in glory. We should walk our pathway in the faith that God knows the best pathway for us, and by His grace He shall lead us to Himself on that path. God is good and desires good for His people.

PRAYER

Dear Lord, give us the grace we need to continue walking that path that leads to You. Put a song of thanksgiving in our hearts. For Jesus' sake. Amen.

JULY 26

"**B**less the Lord, O my soul . . . who redeemeth thy life from destruction; who crowneth thee with lovingkindness and tender mercies" (Ps. 103:2, 4). The believer should meditate on the grace of the Lord in redeeming him from death and hell and providing him all the mercy and grace he needs to walk the life of the believer. It is well for the believer to live his life blessing the Lord for His lovingkindness. Too often we forget to say, "Thank You, Lord," for His constant love and grace. All believers need to cultivate a thankful spirit. As the hymn writer phrased it, we need to count our blessings and thank the Lord for each one.

PRAYER

Thank You, Lord, for all Your blessings. Help me to walk this day with the sense of Your loving care and tender mercies. For Jesus' sake. Amen.

July 27

"**T**rust in the Lord with all thine heart; and lean not unto thine own understanding. In all thy ways acknowledge him, and he shall direct thy paths" (Prov. 3:5–6). The believer needs to trust in the Lord without reservations. God knows our pathway far better than we can. He will guide us by His perfect wisdom into pathways of service and blessing that we cannot imagine. Wholehearted obedience leads to great blessing in the service of God. All believers need guidance in their path of service. God always knows the best path for each believer. We need to ask Him to show us the way.

Prayer

Dear Lord, guide our steps and lead us in paths of blessing and service for You. Give us the strength and grace to follow Your leading. For Jesus' sake. Amen.

JULY 28

"**T**hen shalt thou call, and the Lord shall answer; thou shalt cry, and he shall say, Here I am. . . . And the Lord shall guide thee continually, and satisfy thy soul in drought" (Isa. 58:9, 11). Every believer delights in God's answers to prayer, but often those answers depend on the believer's heart relation with the Lord. He cannot walk willfully in his own path and expect the Lord to overlook his waywardness. He must walk with the Lord on the path that He chooses. Then the Lord will bring His blessings upon him and answer his prayers. The believer must walk the pathway of God's will to have His blessing.

PRAYER

Dear Lord, help us to walk with You along the pathway of Your will for our lives. Give us grace to be a blessing to others on that path. For Jesus' sake. Amen.

JULY 29

"**A**nd unto this people thou shalt say, Thus saith the Lord; Behold, I set before you the way of life, and the way of death" (Jer. 21:8). The Lord commanded the prophet Jeremiah to challenge the people of Israel to choose the will of the Lord, which would lead to life, and to turn away from their own will, which would lead to death. But then as now the people chose selfishly. Their steps were leading to terrible defeat and ultimate deportation. God's will often looks distasteful to God's people, but it is always the best possible pathway for them. We, too, must learn to choose God's will for our lives and to walk humbly with Him.

PRAYER

Dear Lord, guide our steps so that our path draws ever nearer to that home that You have prepared for Your people. For Jesus' sake. Amen.

JULY 30

"**D**epart from evil, and do good; seek peace, and pursue it. The eyes of the Lord are upon the righteous, and his ears are open unto their cry" (Ps. 34:14–15). God's people are not orphans. God is constantly watching over them. They are responsible to turn away from what is evil and to keep on pursuing what they know to be good. God always keeps His promise: "The righteous cry, and the Lord heareth, and delivereth them out of all their troubles" (v. 17). God is infinitely compassionate. He intends complete deliverance and complete victory for His people. They must learn obedience and patient waiting for His deliverance.

PRAYER

Dear Lord, help us to follow Your leading and to seek Your help for every trial we face. Deliver us for Jesus' sake. Amen.

JULY 31

"**A**t midday, O king, I saw in the way a light from heaven, above the brightness of the sun, shining round about me and them which journeyed with me" (Acts 26:13). Paul recounted before King Agrippa his conversion on the Damascus road. His path was certainly contrary to Christ up to that time. But the Lord Jesus appeared to him and completely turned him about and transformed him into a zealous advocate of the gospel. A conversion does not have to be that spectacular, but it must result in a turning about from the things of the world to a dedication to the Lord Jesus Christ. From then on the believer is a pilgrim on the path of the Lord's will for his life.

PRAYER

Lord Jesus, guide our steps on the path of Your will for our lives. Give us the grace we need to live for You. Amen.

AUGUST 1

"**M**y son, give me thine heart, and let thine eyes observe my ways" (Prov. 23:26). Wise King Solomon was a good example to his family. He wanted his children to follow him in the worship and service of God. Parents should ponder this because children do follow the practices and habits they see in their parents. A family that prays together and reads the Bible together has great impact on the lives of the children who grow up in such a family. Children who grow up in a family that is faithful in attending church and active in helpful community projects regularly go on to be leaders in the next generation.

PRAYER

Dear Lord, help me to so live that my life may encourage others to be faithful in service for God and people. For Jesus' sake. Amen.

August 2

"**Y**e have plowed wickedness, ye have reaped iniquity; ye have eaten the fruit of lies: because thou didst trust in thy way, in the multitude of thy mighty men" (Hosea 10:13). A strong army is no protection at all if the Lord removes His hand of protection. The believer must seek the Lord and His righteousness. The prophet invites the believer to seek the Lord and to find His deliverance. "Sow to yourselves in righteousness, reap in mercy; break up your fallow ground: for it is time to seek the Lord, till he come and rain righteousness upon you" (v. 12). Seeking the Lord means turning away from a willful path and walking in the path of the Lord.

PRAYER

Dear Lord, we turn away from trust in ourselves; we trust in Your keeping power. Help us to live for You in the midst of a wicked world. For Jesus' sake. Amen.

AUGUST 3

God "made his own people to go forth like sheep, and guided them in the wilderness like a flock. And he led them on safely, so that they feared not" (Ps. 78:52–53). God led His ancient people out of the bondage of Egypt through a fearsome desert. He was their protection on every hand. God still delivers His people and leads them through the wilderness of this world. It is His holy Word, the Bible, that directs their path. This world is not our home; we are just passing through it. The presence of God in heaven is our eternal home. He alone is able to guide us safely through the dangers of this life. His loving presence will make all the dangers and difficulties of our path worthwhile.

PRAYER

Dear Lord, keep us on the straight and narrow path that leads to Your presence in glory. For Jesus' sake. Amen.

AUGUST 4

Wisdom says, "I lead in the way of righteousness, in the midst of the paths of judgment" (Prov. 8:20). Wisdom leads people in the way of righteousness, the way that God approves. It is significant that the leading is in the midst of the path. Wisdom does not lead to the edge of good judgment, where stumbling is easy, but in the center of the path. The life of the believer should be centered upon the things of God. He must open up a distance between himself and the world, with all its foolish choices. The wise are "those who by reason of use have their senses exercised to discern both good and evil" (Heb. 5:14*b*).

PRAYER

Dear Lord, give us wise discernment that we may walk in the center of Your will, with Your blessing. For Jesus' sake. Amen.

AUGUST 5

"**F**or both prophet and priest are profane. . . . Wherefore their way shall be unto them as slippery ways in the darkness: they shall be driven on, and fall therein: for I will bring evil upon them, even the year of their visitation, saith the Lord" (Jer. 23:11–12). When religious leaders abandon God's standards of conduct, God himself will bring stern judgment upon them. There is no cure for apostasy except judgment. All God's people must walk humbly with Him. Religious leaders have the responsibility to walk closely with the Lord as an example to others. God Himself is watching.

PRAYER

Dear Lord, give us grace to walk with You. Give our pastors and teachers the grace to walk with You and to lead us to You. For Jesus' sake. Amen.

AUGUST 6

"**O** Lord, thou hast searched me, and known me. . . . Thou compassest my path and my lying down, and art acquainted with all my ways" (Ps. 139:1, 3). God knows the path of each believer perfectly. He has a will and a purpose for each one. It is a comfort to every believer that God is guiding his life by providential events and is leading him in a spiritual direction. There are no accidents in the life of a believer. David exclaimed, "How precious also are thy thoughts unto me, O God! how great is the sum of them!" (v. 17). David was sure that God had much more blessing waiting for him. We should walk our pathway with that same confidence of God's care and blessing.

PRAYER

Dear Lord, help us to remember Your purpose for our lives and to walk humbly with You on that path. For Jesus' sake. Amen.

AUGUST 7

"**S**earch me, O God, and know my heart: try me, and know my thoughts: and see if there be any wicked way in me, and lead me in the way everlasting" (Ps. 139:23–24). David prayed that God would search his mind and heart in order to purify him. We all need God's grace to make us what we ought to be. We need God's leading in our lives to bring us to that place of blessing and usefulness to God that we need to be. God's path is never aimless. He intends blessing and service to come to the believer. Walking with God always transforms the believer into something better and greater than he was before. We must walk in that faith.

PRAYER

Dear Lord, help us to walk with You and talk with You along the path of Your will for our lives. Bless us for Jesus' sake. Amen.

AUGUST 8

"**A**nd hast given them this land . . . and they came in, and possessed it; but they obeyed not thy voice, neither walked in thy law; they have done nothing of all that thou commandest them to do: therefore thou hast caused all this evil to come upon them" (Jer. 32:22–23). The prophet Jeremiah speaks in sorrow of the disobedience of his people and warns them of the loss of that land because of their disobedience. There are always consequences for the disobedience of God's Word. In our own day people expect prosperity and pleasure while they are living in ways that violate God's will and His Word. Believers must conform their steps to God's Word and walk in ways that please Him.

PRAYER

Dear Lord, help us to live in ways that reflect our obedience to Your Word. Give us grace to walk with You day by day. For Jesus' sake. Amen.

AUGUST 9

"**B**ut take diligent heed to do the commandment and the law, which Moses the servant of the Lord charged you, to love the Lord your God, and to walk in all his ways, and to cleave unto him, and to serve him with all your heart and with all your soul" (Josh. 22:5). Joshua so exhorted the tribes that had helped subdue the land as they prepared to go back to the east side of Jordan to their own inheritance. Being distant from the center of worship at Jerusalem was a spiritual danger. All believers should keep as close as possible to the church in which they worship God. But their walk with God is always a personal responsibility, not just a corporate gathering. Their heart devotion is central.

PRAYER

Dear Lord, help us to walk with You and to serve You wherever we may be. Draw our hearts to Your presence. For Jesus' sake. Amen.

AUGUST 10

"**I**f thou turn away thy foot . . . from doing thy pleasure . . . and shalt honour him, not doing thine own ways, nor finding thine own pleasure, nor speaking thine own words: then shalt thou delight thyself in the Lord" (Isa. 58:13–14). All people have a habit of pleasing themselves. It takes a deliberate act of will to concentrate on pleasing God rather than self. Isaiah calls upon God's people to turn away from the ways of pleasing themselves and instead to determine to please God with all their heart. That is an act of consecration that brings great blessing into the life of the believer.

PRAYER

Dear Lord, give us grace to please You and to walk in humble obedience to Your will, not our own. For Jesus' sake. Amen.

AUGUST 11

"**A**nd they said one to another, Did not our heart burn within us, while he talked with us by the way, and while he opened to us the scriptures?" (Luke 24:32). The disciples described their encounter with the risen Christ as He explained to them the meaning of His death and resurrection. That is the heart of the gospel. Christ died for our sins and rose again for our justification. All who believe in Him are cleansed from their sins by the power of His blood. We all need to come back to the Scriptures and meditate on the greatness of our salvation in Christ. Let us tell others how we found the Lord Jesus Christ as our Savior.

PRAYER

Thank you, Lord Jesus, for saving us by the shedding of Your blood on the cross. Help us to share our testimony with others. For Your sake. Amen.

AUGUST 12

"**B**y mercy and truth iniquity is purged: and by the fear of the Lord men depart from evil" (Prov. 16:6). Reverence for God causes people to turn away from evil. Iniquity ought to be replaced by mercy and truth. The life of the believer ought to manifest his worship and service for God. People ought to be able to see the difference in his everyday conduct. The proper reverence for God is a protection for the believer in every aspect of his life. Loss of reverence for God leaves the door open for all manner of sin and excess. The fact that God is watching is a governing principle of the believer's life.

PRAYER

Dear Lord, help us to live our lives with the sense of Your presence with us day by day. For Jesus' sake. Amen.

AUGUST 13

Moses prayed to the Lord, "I pray thee, if I have found grace in thy sight, shew me now thy way, that I may know thee, that I may find grace in thy sight" (Exod. 33:13). God did indeed answer Moses' prayer. He led Israel through the wilderness wanderings for forty years. He never failed Moses but always led His people to the right place. The grace of God is always sufficient for every believer. God leads His people along the path of His will for their lives. We need to cultivate the grace of walking humbly with God along the path of His leading. God's holy Word, the Bible, is His guidebook for all who believe.

PRAYER

Dear Lord, open our eyes to the truth of Your Word. Help us to walk with You along the path of Your choosing. For Jesus' sake. Amen.

AUGUST 14

"**Y**et the Lord will command his lovingkindness in the daytime, and in the night his song shall be with me, and my prayer unto the God of my life" (Ps. 42:8). The psalmist walked by faith. He was sure that he would experience the lovingkindness of God as he worked and served God in his daily tasks. He was also sure that in the darkness of night God would be with him to sustain and protect him. His life was wrapped up in prayer to God by day and by night. We need to make God the Lord of our life, by day and by night, trusting in His keeping power. God can put a song in our hearts, even in the darkness of night.

PRAYER

Dear Lord, help us to walk with You by day and by night. Give us grace to live our lives in Your presence. For Jesus' sake. Amen.

August 15

"**T**urn ye again now every one from his evil way, and from the evil of your doings, and dwell in the land that the Lord hath given unto you and to your fathers for ever and ever" (Jer. 25:5). The prophets cried out to their people to forsake their sins and to direct their attention to the worship and service of God. But the people did not listen, and the result was the deportations and captivity that followed. We in our generation are challenged by the words of the prophets. We must forsake our sins and seek to serve the living God from the heart. He will not turn away from those who seek Him with a single-minded heart.

PRAYER

Dear Lord, help us to turn away from what we know is wrong and to seek You with all our heart and soul. For Jesus' sake. Amen.

August 16

"**B**ecause thy lovingkindness is better than life, my lips shall praise thee" (Ps. 63:3). The psalmist was thinking that life in this world lasts just a few years but eternal life in the presence of God will never end. God's lovingkindness upon His people will last for all eternity. The believer should praise God now for eternal life in Christ. The Lord Jesus Christ promised, "Whosoever liveth and believeth in me shall never die" (John 11:26*b*). He was not speaking of physical death but of eternal death. When a person who trusts in Christ dies, he leaves this realm to be with the Lord Jesus. "We are confident . . . and willing rather to be absent from the body, and to be present with the Lord" (2 Cor. 5:8).

PRAYER

Dear Lord, help us to remember Your lovingkindness and to walk with You along life's pathway toward home. For Jesus' sake. Amen.

AUGUST 17

"**Y**e shall walk after the Lord your God . . . and keep his commandments. . . . And that prophet . . . shall be put to death; because he hath spoken to turn you away from the Lord your God" (Deut. 13:4–5). The Lord God takes very seriously any attempt to turn people away from the truth. The right relationship with God is a matter of eternal life or eternal death. You have to live somewhere forever. To live according to the teaching of God's holy Word is to have eternal life. To turn away to any other source of religious truth is to forsake life and all that makes life worth living. The Lord God says, "Repent, and turn yourselves from your idols" (Ezek. 14:6).

PRAYER

Dear Lord, turn our path to You and keep our steps on the straight and narrow pathway. For Jesus' sake. Amen.

AUGUST 18

"**L**et all those that seek thee rejoice and be glad in thee: let such as love thy salvation say continually, The Lord be magnified" (Ps. 40:16). Every believer needs a spirit of rejoicing and thanksgiving. We need to magnify the Lord and His great salvation. At times circumstances can be intimidating, but the believer can always rejoice in the Lord. The psalmist could say, "I am poor and needy; yet the Lord thinketh upon me: thou art my help and my deliverer; make no tarrying, O my God" (v. 17). We need to claim the Lord as our help. He is the One Who can deliver us from all our trials.

PRAYER

Dear Lord, give us grace to rejoice and be glad in You. Help us to think of Your great salvation. For Jesus' sake. Amen.

AUGUST 19

"**I** thought on my ways, and turned my feet unto thy testimonies" (Ps. 119:59). It is a good thing for a believer to think about his pathway and to turn his attention to what the Scriptures say about it. Far too often our steps lead us away from God and His pathway for our lives. We need to ponder our pathway and turn our steps back to ways that please the Lord. His Word teaches us the good way in which to walk that we might please Him and be a blessing to others along the way. We need to remember the words of the psalmist, "Thy word is a lamp unto my feet, and a light unto my path" (Ps. 119:105).

PRAYER

Dear Lord, help us to think about our pathway. Guide our steps into ways that please You and bless Your people. For Jesus' sake. Amen.

AUGUST 20

Moses said to the Israelites, "See, I have set before thee this day life and good . . . in that I command thee this day to love the Lord thy God, to walk in his ways, and to keep his commandments and his statutes and his judgments, that thou mayest live and multiply: and the Lord thy God shall bless thee" (Deut. 30:15–16). Moses showed the Israelites the right path: love toward God and obedience to His Word. Every believer needs to walk humbly with God on the path of His will for his or her life. Obedience to God must always flow from a heart of love and gratitude. God's path is always one of blessing for the believer.

PRAYER

Dear Lord, give us the grace to walk with You on the path of Your will for our lives. For Jesus' sake. Amen.

AUGUST 21

"When thou goest, it shall lead thee; when thou sleepest, it shall keep thee; and when thou awakest, it shall talk with thee. For the commandment is a lamp; and the law is light" (Prov. 6:22–23). God's Word provides guidance and protection for the believer. It illuminates the pathway so that dangers can be avoided and the direction can be certain. All day long the Scripture can speak to the believer, moving him in the right direction, preserving him from stumbling. The believer should hide Scripture in his heart, memorizing the precious words in order that they may comfort and guide him on life's pathway.

PRAYER

Dear Lord, help us to meditate on Your holy Word that it may guide us along the pathway to You. For Jesus' sake. Amen.

AUGUST 22

"**H**e that walketh righteously, and speaketh uprightly; he that despiseth the gain of oppressions, that shaketh his hands from holding of bribes, that stoppeth his ears from hearing of blood, and shutteth his eyes from seeing evil; he shall dwell on high" (Isa. 33:15–16). The prophet makes clear that a good man must turn away from evil. The direction of his life must be toward God. The person who loves to walk with God in this life will get the opportunity to walk with Him throughout eternity. "Thine eyes shall see the king in his beauty: they shall behold the land that is very far off" (Isa. 33:17).

PRAYER

Dear Lord, lead us on the pathway to Yourself. Give us the heart dedication that we need to walk with You. For Jesus' sake. Amen.

AUGUST 23

"**H**ear my voice, O God, in my prayer: preserve my life from fear of the enemy. Hide me from the secret counsel of the wicked" (Ps. 64:1–2). Sometimes we fear the enemy when he is not able to harm us by the providence of God. We must not live in fear but in serene trust in the keeping power of God. The wicked may plot against us in secret, but God can frustrate their evil purposes. A life of humble obedience to God is a testimony to all who know us. God is able to sustain and preserve us. Let us continue talking to the Lord in prayer and living for Him in our daily lives.

PRAYER

Dear Lord, help us to live for You. Preserve us from the plotting of the wicked and help us to trust in You. For Jesus' sake. Amen.

AUGUST 24

"**W**ho is among you that feareth the Lord, that obeyeth the voice of his servant, that walketh in darkness, and hath no light? let him trust in the name of the Lord, and stay upon his God" (Isa. 50:10). The God-fearing believer who faces difficult times should not despair. He may be walking in darkness, but God knows his path and will lead him on the right way. Let him trust in God, for He never abandons His child. The believer should open the pages of the Bible and seek guidance and help from His Word. The Lord Jesus commanded, "Search the scriptures" (John 5:39). That is a path of illumination from God.

PRAYER

Dear Lord, give us the guidance we need. Open our eyes to the truths of Your Word and lead us in the way everlasting. For Jesus' sake. Amen.

AUGUST 25

"**O** that my ways were directed to keep thy statutes! Then shall I not be ashamed" (Ps. 119:5–6). The psalmist feels the shame of knowing the teaching of God's Word and yet of failing to live in obedience to it. We can all sympathize with the psalmist in that regard. We, too, need to put in practice what we know to be God's revealed will. Lack of knowledge is not our problem; lack of consistent obedience to God's Word is. We need to ask the Lord for sustaining grace in order that we may live up to what we know is right. The psalmist prays, "With my whole heart have I sought thee: O let me not wander from thy commandments" (Ps. 119:10).

PRAYER

Dear Lord, give us grace to walk with You in faithful obedience to Your holy Word. For Jesus' sake. Amen.

AUGUST 26

"**H**owbeit when he, the Spirit of truth, is come, he will guide you into all truth: for he shall not speak of himself" (John 16:13). The Spirit of God in the heart of the believer is the true guide of his life. It is the Spirit Who illuminates the Holy Scriptures so that the believer may see the right path before him. It is the Spirit Who guides his steps so that he avoids the snares of the Devil. It is the Spirit Who imparts insight to the believer so that he shuns the deeds of the wicked. It is the Spirit Who leads the believer into pathways of service and blessing. It is the Spirit Who guides the believer all the way home to the presence of God.

PRAYER

Holy Spirit of God, guide my steps this day to honor You and to be a blessing to others. For Jesus' sake. Amen.

AUGUST 27

"**I**f I take the wings of the morning, and dwell in the uttermost parts of the sea; even there shall thy hand lead me, and thy right hand shall hold me" (Ps. 139:9–10). David was sure of the presence and power of God in his life. He trusted in the presence of God with him and the protection of God on his steps. Wherever he was, he trusted in God. We need this same serene trust in the living God. We have our trials to go through and a difficult pathway to walk. God's presence with us makes all the difference. He is our protection and our guide. He will never lead us astray.

PRAYER

Dear Lord, help us to live our lives with the sense of Your presence with us to keep us and to guide us. For Jesus' sake. Amen.

AUGUST 28

"**H**aving therefore, brethren, boldness to enter into the holiest by the blood of Jesus, by a new and living way, which he hath consecrated for us, through the veil, that is to say, his flesh" (Heb. 10:19–20). The death of the Lord Jesus Christ is the atoning sacrifice that opened up the way into the presence of God for the believer. His death paid the price for our sins. Now the believer has access to God through His sacrifice. Believers should come boldly to the throne of grace because Christ's death atoned for their sins. His sacrifice made God our heavenly Father, Who rejoices to hear the prayers of His children.

PRAYER

Dear heavenly Father, thank You for sending Your Son to die for our sins. Help us to live for You and glorify Your name. For Jesus' sake. Amen.

AUGUST 29

"**O** bless our God, ye people, and make the voice of his praise to be heard: which holdeth our soul in life, and suffereth not our feet to be moved" (Ps. 66:8–9). Believers should bless and praise God for all His many benefits. He is the One Who keeps our soul alive and preserves our feet from stumbling. We need to look to Him for protection and guidance in our lives. Others need to hear how much God does for His people. The psalmist could say, "Come and hear, all ye that fear God, and I will declare what he hath done for my soul" (Ps. 66:16). We need to testify what He has done for our souls as well.

PRAYER

Dear Lord, thank You for Your countless blessings and daily protection. Help us to remember to praise You for all Your goodness to us. Amen.

August 30

"The Lord shall establish thee an holy people unto himself . . . if thou shalt keep the commandments of the Lord thy God, and walk in his ways" (Deut. 28:9). God promised to bless the Israelites if they would live obediently in the ways He commanded. Of course they did not obey, and He had to bring judgment upon them. But this passage gives us a clear picture of the responsibility that believers have to live in obedience to God's revealed Word. We have much more light than the old Israelites had. We have the completed Scriptures to illumine our pathway. We need to live in obedience to the whole Word of God by His grace.

Prayer

Dear Lord, help us to live according to Your Word and to walk in ways that please You. For Jesus' sake. Amen.

AUGUST 31

"**A**nd David behaved himself wisely in all his ways; and the Lord was with him" (1 Sam. 18:14). David had to face the jealousy of King Saul over his victories on the battlefield. Day by day he had to live wisely in order to keep Saul from his angry plots. But the Lord preserved David again and again from the snares of King Saul. We, too, need the protection of the Lord from the suspicions of worldly people about us. We need to walk in wisdom day by day. But we may be sure that the Lord is with us, just as He was with David during those difficult days. The Lord will never abandon His people.

PRAYER

Dear Lord, help us to live wisely in the sight of worldly people. Preserve our steps from the attacks of others. For Jesus' sake. Amen.

SEPTEMBER 1

"O give thanks unto the Lord; for he is good: for his mercy endureth for ever. . . . To him which led his people through the wilderness: for his mercy endureth for ever" (Ps. 136:1, 16). The Lord led His people through the wilderness for forty years and brought them safely to the Promised Land. We need to remember the goodness of the Lord in leading us through the wilderness of the world and bringing us to the light of His Word. We have victory over worldly strongholds through the grace that is in Christ Jesus. We can be sure that He will lead us to His promised city above by the grace of the Lord Jesus Christ.

PRAYER

Dear Lord, help us to see the leading of Your Word and to walk faithfully on the pathway of Your will for our lives. For Jesus' sake. Amen.

SEPTEMBER 2

The Lord invited Solomon to ask for a divine gift. Solomon mentioned his father David, who walked before God in truth (1 Kings 3:6), and prayed, "Give therefore thy servant an understanding heart to judge thy people" (1 Kings 3:9). God was pleased with his prayer and said, "Lo, I have given thee a wise and an understanding heart. . . . And if thou wilt walk in my ways, to keep my statutes and my commandments, as thy father David did walk, then I will lengthen thy days" (1 Kings 3:12, 14). Solomon was the wisest king, but we all need the wisdom of God to fulfill His purpose in our lives.

PRAYER

Dear Lord, give us the wisdom we need for our daily walk before You. Help us to choose wisely that our lives may please You. For Jesus' sake. Amen.

SEPTEMBER 3

"**T**he highway of the upright is to depart from evil: he that keepeth his way preserveth his soul" (Prov. 16:17). The proper direction of life is away from evil and toward God. Life does not stand still. The believer must make sure that his life is drawing ever closer to God and His will. The person who does not guard his way will soon find his steps slipping. The highway of God's people is always the way marked out in God's holy Word. The Scriptures teach us the good way that will bring us to the presence of God and eternal blessing. We need to walk with faithful submission on His way.

PRAYER

Dear Lord, help us to walk with You on the pathway of Your will for our lives. For Jesus' sake. Amen.

September 4

The Lord has gracious words for Israel: "I will heal their backsliding, I will love them freely: for mine anger is turned away from him. I will be as the dew unto Israel" (Hosea 14:4–5). God will graciously restore His people. His blessing will rest upon them as the dew. Today God's grace in Christ heals the backsliding of God's people. The blessing of God rests upon believers as the dew. The love of God in Christ is the source of blessing and strength for all of God's people. We need to live our lives with the sense of His presence and blessing upon us. We need to learn to walk with God through life.

Prayer

Thank You, dear Lord, for Your love to us in Christ. Help us to walk with You on our pilgrim pathway homeward. For Jesus' sake. Amen.

SEPTEMBER 5

"I thought on my ways, and turned my feet unto thy testimonies" (Ps. 119:59). Everyone needs to think about the pathway he is traveling through this world. Many are traveling in the wrong direction. The psalmist thought on his ways and turned to the guidance of Scripture. God's Word is the only safe guide through life. The teaching of Scripture can protect us from stumbling into paths of danger and corruption. It can lead us into paths of service and blessing that will honor God and provide help for people. We need to turn to the Scriptures and search them in order to find the pathway of blessing that God wishes to bring into our lives.

PRAYER

Dear Lord, show us the path of Your will for our lives. Guide us by Your Word into pathways of blessing. For Jesus' sake. Amen.

SEPTEMBER 6

"The way of peace they know not; and there is no judgment in their goings: they have made them crooked paths: whosoever goeth therein shall not know peace" (Isa. 59:8). The prophet speaks sternly against the iniquities of his people. They are not walking in the way of peace as God has commanded. There is no justice in their pathways. "We wait for light . . . but we walk in darkness" (Isa. 59:9). God's people need to turn their backs on the crooked paths and walk in the light as God has commanded. The Lord Jesus promised, "I am the light of the world: he that followeth me shall not walk in darkness, but shall have the light of life" (John 8:12b).

PRAYER

Dear Lord, rescue us from the darkness of crooked paths and help us to walk with You in paths of light. For Jesus' sake. Amen.

SEPTEMBER 7

Jeremiah gives a stern warning to his people: "Because my people have forgotten me, they have burned incense to vanity, and they have caused them to stumble in their ways from the ancient paths. . . . I will scatter them as with an east wind before the enemy" (Jer. 18:15, 17). Many in our own day forget the Lord and stumble from the ancient paths and find themselves overwhelmed by circumstances they cannot overcome. They need to return to the paths of the Lord and to walk humbly before Him. He can guide them to paths of blessing and service. We must never forget God.

PRAYER

Dear Lord, help us to remember to walk humbly with You on the ancient paths that lead to blessing and service. For Jesus' sake. Amen.

SEPTEMBER 8

Ezekiel warns his people, "Therefore I will judge you, O house of Israel, every one according to his ways, saith the Lord God. Repent, and turn yourselves from all your transgressions; so iniquity shall not be your ruin" (Ezek. 18:30). This is a stern reminder that sin and iniquity ruin people. There are many different ways in which people may depart from the Lord. But every one of them will ruin the people who do so. It is the presence of the Lord that keeps and preserves His people. We need to cherish the presence of the Lord and to walk faithfully with Him.

PRAYER

Dear Lord, help us to be conscious of Your presence with us. Enable us to walk in ways that please You. For Jesus' sake. Amen.

SEPTEMBER 9

"**S**pots they are and blemishes . . . which hath forsaken the right way, and are gone astray, following the way of Balaam the son of Bosor, who loved the wages of unrighteousness" (2 Pet. 2:13, 15). The apostle Peter warns against false teachers and holds up a negative example, the mercenary prophet Balaam, who prophesied what people wanted to hear. The believer must testify to what God has revealed in His Word, the Bible. The Scripture is the Word of truth that sets the prisoner free from sin and error. We must believe the Bible to be set free to walk the right way, the way that leads to God.

PRAYER

Dear Lord, close our ears to false teachers and help us to center our attention on Your holy Word, the Bible. For Jesus' sake. Amen.

SEPTEMBER 10

"**T**hough I walk in the midst of trouble, thou wilt revive me . . . and thy right hand shall save me" (Ps. 138:7). The believer is often surrounded by trouble. David certainly had his share, but he was sure of the presence and protection of God. He expected the mighty hand of God to rescue him. He was walking according to God's Word, trusting God to protect him from his adversaries. In the same way the believer today needs to live his life with the faith that God will preserve him and guide him through His holy Word. God can protect him from the trouble around him. He can walk through trouble in serene peace.

PRAYER

Dear Lord, give us that confident trust in Your keeping power. Help us to walk according to Your Word. For Jesus' sake. Amen.

SEPTEMBER 11

Solomon said, "Hear, O my son, and receive my sayings; and the years of thy life shall be many. I have taught thee in the way of wisdom; I have led thee in right paths" (Prov. 4:10–11). Solomon taught his son wisely in the hope that he would live many years in peace. However, his heirs did not follow in his wisdom. We ought to take his words of wisdom very seriously. Wise conduct leads to years of blessing. God alone has supreme wisdom, as Paul writes, "To God only wise, be glory through Jesus Christ for ever. Amen" (Rom. 16:27). We ought to seek the wisdom of God that we may please Him in all things.

PRAYER

Dear Lord, give us the wisdom we need to walk with You and obey Your Word in our daily lives. For Jesus' sake. Amen.

SEPTEMBER 12

David writes concerning those who hear the words of the Lord, "Yea, they shall sing in the ways of the Lord: for great is the glory of the Lord" (Ps. 138:5). God's people should indeed sing as they walk the ways of the Lord. David sang praise to the Lord "for thy lovingkindness and for thy truth: for thou hast magnified thy word above all thy name" (Ps. 138:2). The psalmist declares, "The Lord is high above all nations, and his glory above the heavens" (Ps. 113:4). Believers have the privilege of worshiping the Lord of the universe. We should seize the opportunity and worship the Lord of heaven and earth.

PRAYER

Dear Lord, we praise You for Your greatness and Your love for Your people. Help us to serve You from the heart. For Jesus' sake. Amen.

SEPTEMBER 13

"But the path of the just is as the shining light, that shineth more and more unto the perfect day" (Prov. 4:18). When a person walks with God, his path gets brighter and brighter day by day. There is a stronger comfort in knowing that God is always with him. The assurance grows that God is guiding him day by day on a path that leads to Himself. The difficulties of the way are not stumbling stones; they are steppingstones toward God. In contrast "the way of the wicked is as darkness: they know not at what they stumble" (Prov. 4:19). How gracious is the Lord in guiding His people to Himself!

PRAYER

Dear Lord, help us to sense Your presence with us as we walk Your way in humble obedience to Your will. For Jesus' sake. Amen.

SEPTEMBER 14

Isaiah writes of future millennial blessings. "The redeemed shall walk there: and the ransomed of the Lord shall return, and come to Zion with songs and everlasting joy upon their heads: they shall obtain joy and gladness, and sorrow and sighing shall flee away" (Isa. 35:9–10). God's people can have a foretaste of such blessings in their daily walk with God. God listens to their prayers. They have the privilege of walking with God in their daily life. He is with them every step of the way. We must walk by faith and commune with Him every step of the way. Let us praise Him for such a privilege.

PRAYER

Dear Lord, we thank You for the privilege of Your presence with us day by day. Keep us on the right path. For Jesus' sake. Amen.

SEPTEMBER 15

God promises to restore His people to the land. "Behold, I will gather them out of all countries, whither I have driven them . . . and I will bring them again unto this place, and I will cause them to dwell safely: and they shall be my people, and I will be their God: and I will give them one heart, and one way" (Jer. 32:37–39). But they must turn to Him. He invites them, "Call unto me, and I will answer thee, and shew thee great and mighty things, which thou knowest not" (Jer. 33:3). It would be well for all men to repent of their willfulness and to turn to God and call upon Him for their salvation.

PRAYER

Dear God, rescue us from the downward path and turn our steps to You. Give us grace to walk with You. For Jesus' sake. Amen.

SEPTEMBER 16

Jonah's preaching was "Let them turn every one from his evil way. . . . And God saw their works, that they turned from their evil way; and God repented of the evil" (Jon. 2:8, 10). Jonah's preaching led to a remarkable revival in ancient Nineveh. They were a cruel and ruthless people, but God's message changed them. They turned from the evil of their way to obedience to God's Word. God spared the whole city because of the faithful preaching of one of His servants. This is a reminder to us all to be faithful witnesses for God. Who knows what God's Word may accomplish though us?

PRAYER

Dear God, help us to share Your Word with the lost that they also may have the chance to hear and believe. For Jesus' sake. Amen.

SEPTEMBER 17

"**B**e ye not as your fathers, unto whom the former prophets have cried, saying, Thus saith the Lord of hosts; Turn ye now from your evil ways, and from your evil doings: but they did not hear, nor hearken unto me, saith the Lord" (Zech. 1:4). Past generations may have failed in seeking God, but that is no excuse for the people in the present generation to fail in the same way. We need to turn away from our evil doings and listen to the teaching of God's holy Word. We should not merely try to avoid evil things, but instead we should positively fill our thoughts with the powerful teaching of God's Word in order that it may empower a life of service and victory for us.

PRAYER

Dear Lord, enable us to fill our minds with Your holy Word in order that we may become a help to others on the pilgrim path. For Jesus' sake. Amen.

SEPTEMBER 18

"**B**ut my words and my statutes, which I commanded my servants the prophets, did they not take hold of your fathers? and they returned and said, Like as the Lord of hosts thought to do unto us, according to our ways, and according to our doings, so hath he dealt with us" (Zech. 1:6). We in our generation can think back to how God's Word took hold of D. L. Moody and Billy Sunday and transformed them into powerful preachers. Now it is our place to listen to the Word of God and to allow it to transform us into servants of the Lord in our time. Are we too busy listening to the clamor of the world to hear the Word of the living God?

PRAYER

Dear Lord, give us a hunger for Your Word that we may fill our minds with its teaching and allow it to guide our steps. For Jesus' sake. Amen.

SEPTEMBER 19

At the dedication of the temple Solomon prayed, "Lord God of Israel, there is no God like thee, in heaven above, or on earth beneath, who keepest covenant and mercy with thy servants that walk before thee with all their heart" (1 Kings 8:23). Heaven and earth are not a committee project. The one true God has made it all. Now it is our responsibility to walk before God with all our heart. We need His mercy and grace in Christ to accomplish His will. The same God Who was merciful in Solomon's day is merciful today to all who pray to Him, but the responsibility of a wholehearted walk before Him is also ours.

PRAYER

Dear Lord, give us grace to walk before You with all our heart. Help us to please You day by day. For Jesus' sake. Amen.

SEPTEMBER 20

"**W**hile I live will I praise the Lord: I will sing praises unto my God while I have any being" (Ps. 146:2). The psalmist was determined to praise God as long as he had any being. He was sure that "the Lord loveth the righteous" (Ps. 146:8). The psalmist responded with praise and celebration for the goodness of God. It is a good thing for all believers to remember to praise God for His goodness to His people. Some people are complainers, but the people of God ought to be praisers of God for the multitude of His blessings. "Happy is he that hath the God of Jacob for his help, whose hope is in the Lord his God" (Ps. 146:5).

PRAYER

Dear Lord, put Your song in the hearts of Your people that we may be praising Your name. For Jesus' sake. Amen.

SEPTEMBER 21

"**S**he [wisdom] is a tree of life to them that lay hold upon her: and happy is every one that retaineth her" (Prov. 3:18). This was written from a dry and thirsty land in which the possession of a fig tree or olive tree was the difference between life and death. Wisdom sustains the people who draw upon her. The lack of wisdom destroys people. A wise person avoids harmful things and dangerous pathways. The foolish person blunders into disaster that harms him and others. The wise person chooses a pathway that God will bless; the foolish person chooses a path that God must judge. We must all ponder the consequences of our choices.

PRAYER

Dear Lord, help us to choose wisely the path we walk. Guide us in our steps that we may please You and bless others. For Jesus' sake. Amen.

SEPTEMBER 22

"**T**hus saith God the Lord, he that created the heavens . . . he that spread forth the earth . . . he that giveth breath unto the people upon it, and spirit to them that walk therein: I the Lord have called thee in righteousness" (Isa. 42:5–6). Here the Lord speaks to "my servant" (v. 1), Who is to be "a light of the Gentiles; to open the blind eyes, to bring out the prisoners from the prison" (vv. 6–7). This is a great messianic prophecy of the ministry of the Lord Jesus Christ. He alone has the power to free people from their sins and bring them to the heavenly Father. We should give thanks to Him for the salvation He so freely imparts.

PRAYER

Thank You, Lord, for the salvation that You have provided for those who trust in the great Messiah, the Lord Jesus Christ. Amen.

September 23

"**I** sought for a man among them, that should make up the hedge, and stand in the gap before me for the land . . . but I found none. Therefore have I poured out mine indignation upon them . . . their own way have I recompensed upon their heads, saith the Lord God" (Ezek. 22:30–31). Where can the Lord find a person who will lead His people back into ways of righteousness? There was no one in the days of Ezekiel. The Lord had to bring judgment upon His people to awake them to their sins. In our own day the Lord brings disaster upon people to awake them of their need of His grace and forgiveness. We must stand against the iniquity of our day.

PRAYER

Dear Lord, give us grace to stand for You against the iniquity of our own day. Deliver us from evil for Jesus' sake. Amen.

SEPTEMBER 24

"**S**earch me, O God . . . and see if there be any wicked way in me, and lead me in the way everlasting" (Ps. 139:23–24). The way of God's will is the way everlasting. God's perfect will never changes. We, however, are quick to change our path to a more worldly one. We need the guidance of God to the path of His perfect will for our lives. We can fulfill God's purpose for our lives only by continuing along the path He marks out for us. There are always great blessings in his path. It may be difficult, but there is great comfort in knowing that His way is everlasting fellowship with God.

PRAYER

Dear Lord, lead me in that everlasting way. Protect me from evil and help me to walk with you every step of the way. For Jesus' sake. Amen.

September 25

Solomon said, "My son, attend to my words. . . . For they are life unto those that find them, and health to all their flesh. Keep thy heart with all diligence; for out of it are the issues of life" (Prov. 4:20, 22–23). Words of wisdom are life to those who treasure them. We must all diligently guard our heart, for our heart attitude settles the direction of our life. A wicked person has a wrong heart attitude before he does outward wrongs. A person who has a right heart relationship with God is going to live right, even in difficult situations. God will strengthen his heart to live for Him.

Prayer

Dear Lord, warm our hearts and draw us close to You. Give us grace to live for You in the midst of life's trials. For Jesus' sake. Amen.

SEPTEMBER 26

"When thou passest through the waters, I will be with thee; and through the rivers, they shall not overflow thee: when thou walkest through the fire, thou shalt not be burned; neither shall the flame kindle upon thee. For I am the Lord thy God" (Isa. 43:2–3). God's people often have trials they must pass through, but they never have to face them alone. In every trial the Lord is with His people to sustain and deliver them. We must trust Him to bring us safely through the trials of life. He intends them for good. They cause us to draw near to Him for grace and help. His presence can turn trials into blessings.

PRAYER

Dear Lord, help us to see Your hand in the midst of every trial. Give us grace to reach out to You for help in every time of need. For Jesus' sake. Amen.

SEPTEMBER 27

"**H**ave ye forgotten the wickedness of your fathers . . . and your own wickedness. . . . They are not humbled even unto this day, neither have they feared" (Jer. 44:9–10). People forget the hardening effect of sins persisted in and repeated day after day. They need to repent of their sins and forsake them. God can forgive them of their sins and transform them into faithful servants of righteousness through the blood of Christ. He died to set men free from their sins and to enable them to live for Him. People need to ask Him for forgiveness and cleansing from their sins. Christ "is able also to save them to the uttermost that come unto God by him" (Heb. 7:25).

PRAYER

Dear Lord, forgive us of our sins by the merits of the Lord Jesus Christ. Make us servants of Him by Your grace. Amen.

SEPTEMBER 28

"**A** wise man feareth, and departeth from evil: but the fool rageth, and is confident" (Prov. 14:16). When a wise man encounters evil, he turns and gets away from it as fast as he can. But when a fool encounters evil, he is confident that he is more than able to conquer all opposition. A wise man recognizes his weaknesses and seeks grace and help from the Lord. The Lord is always able to help the seeking soul, but a fool does not know that he needs God and tries to solve his problems by force and fury. A wise man walks humbly with God on a path that leads away from evil to a life of blessing.

PRAYER

Dear Lord, give us grace and wisdom to walk with You through this wicked world. For Jesus' sake. Amen.

SEPTEMBER 29

"**I** will bring the blind by a way that they knew not; I will lead them in paths that they have not known: I will make darkness light before them, and crooked things straight. These things will I do unto them, and not forsake them" (Isa. 42:16). Isaiah prophesies the ministry of Messiah, the servant of the Lord. Matthew refers to this passage when he describes the Galilean ministry of the Lord Jesus Christ (Matt. 12:15–21). He is the One Who can turn our darkness into light and can lead us in paths of God's blessing. We need to put our trust in Him and humbly follow His leading.

PRAYER

Thank You, dear Lord, for caring for us and for leading us in paths of righteousness. Give us obedient hearts. For Jesus' sake. Amen.

SEPTEMBER 30

Wisdom personified cries out, "For whoso findeth me findeth life, and shall obtain favour of the Lord. But he that sinneth against me wrongeth his own soul" (Prov. 8:35–36). People who act unwisely are harming their own selves. On the other hand people who act wisely are helping themselves and benefiting others as well. People who make foolish choices ruin their own lives and make life difficult for others. Every person's life has a "ripple effect" on the lives of those around him. Each of us needs to make sure that our lives have an effect for good on all those around us.

PRAYER

Dear Lord, help us to live so that our lives may be a blessing to those around us. For Jesus' sake. Amen.

OCTOBER 1

"**I** therefore, the prisoner of the Lord, beseech you that ye walk worthy of the vocation wherewith ye are called, with all lowliness and meekness, with longsuffering, forbearing one another in love" (Eph. 4:1–2). The apostle Paul left a good example for believers to follow by enduring persecution and trials with patience. We all need to exercise the lowliness and meekness that Paul encouraged and manifested. He was longsuffering in his trials. We need to follow him in forbearing one another in Christian love. God calls all of us to live our lives in ways that bring Him honor and glory.

PRAYER

Dear Lord, give us grace to live our lives in meekness and longsuffering, walking in love as You do toward us. For Jesus' sake. Amen.

OCTOBER 2

"Thou hast avouched the Lord this day to be thy God, and to walk in his ways, and to keep his statutes, and his commandments, and his judgments, and to hearken unto his voice" (Deut. 26:17). The Israelites had pledged themselves to obey the Lord and his Word to them. We have a solemn Word of the Lord in the Bible that we need to obey and follow. In our hearts we need to commit ourselves to obey the Word of the Lord and to live our lives in the light of the Bible and its teaching. Obeying the Word of the Lord is always the pathway to spiritual blessing for believers.

PRAYER

Dear Lord, help us to be obedient to the teaching of Your holy Word to us. Enable us to serve You from the heart. For Jesus' sake. Amen.

OCTOBER 3

The Lord God said to Solomon, "If thou wilt walk before me, as David thy father walked, in integrity of heart, and in uprightness . . . then I will establish the throne of thy kingdom upon Israel for ever" (1 Kings 9:4–5). In his early years Solomon served the Lord with uprightness of heart and experienced great blessing upon his reign, but in later years his many foreign wives "turned away his heart after other gods" (1 Kings 11:4). Solomon soon found adversaries in the surrounding kingdoms. We must serve the Lord with singleness of heart to experience His blessing upon our lives.

PRAYER

Dear Lord, help us to serve You with single-minded devotion. Give us a servant's heart. For Jesus' sake. Amen.

OCTOBER 4

"Let all those that seek thee rejoice and be glad in thee: and let such as love thy salvation say continually, Let God be magnified" (Ps. 70:4). Seeking God is the most joyous thing people can do in this life. The frothy pleasures of modern life soon disappear, but the joy of the presence of God never disappears. People who love God's salvation have joy welling up within their souls constantly. They need to be thinking of how they can magnify God in their lives. God has put them in the place they find themselves so that they may be a testimony to Him to all that know them.

PRAYER

Dear Lord, help us to live for You in the midst of the busy activities of life. Give us the joy of Your presence with us. For Jesus' sake. Amen.

OCTOBER 5

"Let us search and try our ways, and turn again to the Lord. Let us lift up our heart with our hands unto God in the heavens" (Lam. 3:40–41). The remnant after the fall of Jerusalem mourned over their desolate condition. They thought of God in the heavens and lifted up their hands in petition to Him. We, too, need to turn to God in times of trouble. We need to forsake the sins that destroyed us and turn to God, Who can forgive and restore us. We should lift up our hearts to God in heaven, Who can open up ways of restoration and avenues of service. His hand is not shortened that it cannot reach us. Let us call upon Him in faith.

PRAYER

O Lord, have mercy upon us. Deliver us from sin and selfishness. Lead us to paths of blessing and fellowship with You. For Jesus' sake. Amen.

OCTOBER 6

"Woe unto us, that we have sinned! . . . Turn thou us unto thee, O Lord, and we shall be turned; renew our days as of old" (Lam. 5:16, 21). God in His grace can turn us from darkness to His light. There is forgiveness and restoration in His Son, the Lord Jesus Christ. The Lord Jesus invited us, "Come unto me, all ye that labour and are heavy laden, and I will give you rest. Take my yoke upon you, and learn of me" (Matt. 11:28–29). The Lord Jesus is the Savior of all who call upon Him in truth. His blood can wash away our sins and turn us to paths of righteousness.

PRAYER

O Lord, forgive us our sins for Jesus' sake. Turn us to paths of blessing and service for You according to Your promises. For Jesus' sake. Amen.

OCTOBER 7

"**B**lessed is every one that feareth the Lord; that walketh in his ways" (Ps. 128:1). God's blessing rests on every one who reverences Him. "Walking in his ways" refers to living a life that reflects the way of the Lord that Scripture teaches. Obedience to God's Word always brings blessing and spiritual benefits to believers. Reverence for God is rare in the modern world. The world needs to see believers who are truly dedicated to God and who will live for him in the midst of this wicked world. God's blessing will rest upon those faithful believers.

PRAYER

Dear Lord, help us to live for You with reverence and obedience to Your Word. Give us grace and courage. For Jesus' sake. Amen.

OCTOBER 8

"The righteous perisheth, and no man layeth it to heart . . . none considering that the righteous is taken away from the evil to come. He shall enter into peace" (Isa. 57:1–2). The death of a person who is right with God is not a tragedy. He is taken away from further suffering in this life and is in perfect peace in the presence of God. The wicked are left to endure further trials here unless they repent. The death of a righteous person is not a tragedy but a home going to the presence of the God he served in this life. His joyous service in the presence of God will never end.

PRAYER

Dear Lord, help us to understand that submission to Your Word in this life leads to eternal joy in Your presence in the next. For Jesus' sake. Amen.

OCTOBER 9

"**I** have sent also unto you all my servants the prophets, rising up early and sending them, saying, Return ye now every man from his evil way, and amend your doings, and go not after other gods to serve them, and ye shall dwell in the land . . . but ye have not inclined your ear, nor hearkened unto me" (Jer. 35:15). The Lord warned His people of their need for obedience to His Word, but they would not listen. In our day people go their own way, heedless of the warnings of Scripture, and then wonder why catastrophe overtakes them. We all need to ponder our pathway and turn our steps into obedience to God's holy Word.

PRAYER

Dear Lord, open our eyes to the teaching of Your Word and help us to walk in ways that please You. For Jesus' sake. Amen.

OCTOBER 10

"**A**nd ye shall know that I am the Lord, when I shall bring you into the land of Israel. . . . And there shall ye remember your ways, and all your doings, wherein ye have been defiled" (Ezek. 20:42–43). The Lord warned His earthly people that He would deliver them and bring them back into their land, but there they should remember their evil deeds that brought about their captivity. We must all remember that sin brings consequences and often sorrow later on. We need to ask the Lord for grace to forsake sin and live for Him in this life. A defiled believer is an unhappy person; we need to seek the Lord for forgiveness and cleansing that the joy of the Lord may be ours.

Prayer

Dear Lord, cleanse us from the sins of the past that we may walk with You in a life of humble obedience. For Jesus' sake. Amen.

OCTOBER 11

"**O** thou that art named the house of Jacob, is the spirit of the Lord straitened? are these his doings? do not my words do good to him that walketh uprightly?" (Mic. 2:7). The stern rebukes of Scripture are beneficial to those who read them. They move the reader away from evil and toward the good. The teachings of Scripture move the reader to obey God and to be a blessing to others. They show the reader how to live so as to be a person guided by the Spirit of the Lord. The words of Scripture are a source of blessing and benefit to every serious reader. The Lord Jesus commanded, "Search the scriptures" (John 5:39). We should obey that command every day.

PRAYER

Dear Lord, put a hunger in our souls for Your holy Word. Give us strength and blessing each day as we read. For Jesus' sake. Amen.

OCTOBER 12

The Lord said to Jeroboam, "Behold, I will rend the kingdom out of the hand of Solomon . . . because that they have forsaken me . . . and have not walked in my ways, to do that which is right in mine eyes, and to keep my statutes and my judgments, as did David his father" (1 Kings 11:31, 33). There are always consequences for sin. Solomon's heir, Rehoboam, lost ten tribes because of the worship of false gods, Ashtoreth, Chemosh, and Milcom. God's people must always beware lest some idol take their attention away from the one true God. In our day the idol may not be a graven image, but it may be something worshiped, nonetheless. We need single-minded devotion to God alone.

PRAYER

Dear Lord, help us to forsake every idol and to worship and serve You alone. For Jesus' sake. Amen.

OCTOBER 13

"**T**hus shall the man be blessed that feareth the Lord. The Lord shall bless thee out of Zion: and thou shalt see the good of Jerusalem all the days of thy life" (Ps. 128:4–5). Reverence for God brings blessing into the life of the believer. God sees the heart devotion of the believer and blesses his life and labors. Each believer should live his life consciously in the presence of God. He needs to walk with God each day of his life that God may use him as an instrument of blessing and benefit to others. True happiness does not come from idleness but from the labor of love for the Lord and for others.

PRAYER

Dear Lord, give us that reverence for You that will make us a blessing to others. For Jesus' sake. Amen.

OCTOBER 14

"**H**e that walketh in his uprightness feareth the Lord: but he that is perverse in his ways despiseth him" (Prov. 14:2). A person who lives an upright, godly life demonstrates that he reverences God and His Word. On the other hand a person who lives a wicked, reckless life shows that he has no respect for the will and law of God. The lifestyle manifests the inward character of the person. Every believer must be careful to live a life that clearly manifests his devotion to God and His Word. Others are reading his devotion from the actions of his life. A walk with God is a blessing to all.

PRAYER

Dear Lord, help us to walk with You day by day. Give us the grace we need to be a blessing to others. For Jesus' sake. Amen.

OCTOBER 15

"**T**hen shalt thou call, and the Lord shall answer; thou shalt cry, and he shall say, Here I am. . . . And they that shall be of thee shall build the old waste places: thou shalt raise up the foundations of many generations; and thou shalt be called, The repairer of the breach, The restorer of paths to dwell in" (Isa. 58:9, 12). Praying to the Lord brings great help and blessing. The Lord's answer may impart more blessing than you asked for. Your praying and your devotion may make you a restorer of godly living and testimony. God's blessing may continue your service to others for generations.

PRAYER

Dear Lord, help me to serve You well. Grant that my service for You will be a help to others in their service as well. For Jesus' sake. Amen.

OCTOBER 16

The leaders of the remnant came to Jeremiah and said, "Pray for us unto the Lord thy God, even for all this remnant . . . that the Lord thy God may shew us the way wherein we may walk, and the thing that we may do" (Jer. 42:2–3). Jeremiah recounted to them the word of the Lord, that they should stay in the land and the Lord would be with them, but they refused to listen and fled to Egypt for safety. They did not want the Lord's direction; they wanted His approval on their plans. People still try to pull God around to approve what they want rather than obeying the Word of God. It never works.

PRAYER

Dear Lord, give us the grace to obey Your Word and not to try to twist it around to what we want. Give us an obedient heart. For Jesus' sake. Amen.

OCTOBER 17

"When I say unto the wicked, O wicked man, thou shalt surely die; if thou dost not speak to warn the wicked from his way, that wicked man shall die in his iniquity; but his blood will I require at thine hand" (Ezek. 33:8). The wicked need to hear the warnings in God's Word that may make them turn from their wicked ways. If believers keep a guilty silence, they are allowing the wicked to stumble on into disaster and perdition. They need to hear, even if they do not want the message. The believer does not have to be popular, just faithful to God. If God is pleased, that is enough.

PRAYER

Dear Lord, give us the courage to stand on Your side and faithfully tell others their need of repentance and conversion. For Jesus' sake. Amen.

OCTOBER 18

"**N**evertheless, if thou warn the wicked of his way to turn from it; if he do not turn from his way, he shall die in his iniquity; but thou hast delivered thy soul" (Ezek. 33:9). The believer must do what is right whether people like it or not. If they will not heed a warning, at least the believer has a good conscience. He has done what is right. And the individual may think about what he has heard and reconsider. Many people have spurned good advice but have thought about it and decided that, after all, they should follow it. Sowing the seed of God's Word can bring forth an eternal harvest.

PRAYER

Dear Lord, help us to be faithful in sowing the seed of the Word. Grant that it may bring forth eternal fruit. For Jesus' sake. Amen.

OCTOBER 19

"**S**ay unto them, As I live, saith the Lord God, I have no pleasure in the death of the wicked; but that the wicked turn from his way and live: turn ye, turn ye from your evil ways; for why will ye die, O house of Israel?" (Ezek. 33:11). God's desire for people is that they turn from their wicked ways and live for Him. They are not only honoring God by such repentance but they are rescuing themselves from a life of sin and shame. The wages of sin are always death. But God desires people to forsake sin and to live with His blessing. Pleasing God is an eternal blessing as well as salvation.

PRAYER

Dear Lord, turn our steps to You and enable us to walk with You on the right path of life. For Jesus' sake. Amen.

OCTOBER 20

"**F**or it had been better for them not to have known the way of righteousness, than, after they have known it, to turn from the holy commandment delivered unto them" (2 Pet. 2:21). Spiritual ignorance is better than willful rejection of the truth. But better yet is Peter's exhortation to "be mindful of the words which were spoken before by the holy prophets, and of the commandment of us the apostles of the Lord and Saviour" (2 Pet. 3:2*b*). To walk the way of righteousness is a blessed privilege for believers. They never walk alone, for the Lord is always with them.

PRAYER

Dear Lord, help us to walk with You on the way of righteousness. Guide our steps homeward to Your presence in glory. For Jesus' sake. Amen.

OCTOBER 21

"**A**nd the priest said unto them, Go in peace: before the Lord is your way wherein ye go" (Judg. 18:6). Although the way of the Danites was not peace, but rather war, the priest was correct in saying that their way was before the Lord. God observes the way of every person. He sees whether it is a good way or an evil way. It is well for all people to remember that God is the observer of all human actions and that He knows the motives of the human heart. No one can deceive Him. We should all walk humbly before Him and seek His peace and blessing upon our lives. He alone can cause our way to prosper.

PRAYER

Dear Lord, help us to walk in the consciousness of your presence with us. Give us guidance and help on our pathway. For Jesus' sake. Amen.

OCTOBER 22

"**O**pen to me the gates of righteousness: I will go into them, and I will praise the Lord: this gate of the Lord, into which the righteous shall enter" (Ps. 118:19–20). The psalmist prayed that the Lord would open to him the gates of righteousness that he might live for the Lord. We too need to pray that the Lord will direct our steps into paths of righteousness. Our lives ought to be testimonies to the Lord's guidance and blessing. We too ought to praise the Lord for His hand of blessing on our lives. We need to live for Him this day and seek to be a blessing to others as well. We should praise the Lord for our opportunities of service and testimony.

PRAYER

Dear Lord, thank You for Your gifts to Your people. Help us to testify of Your goodness and mercy. For Jesus' sake. Amen.

OCTOBER 23

"**M**ake me to go in the path of thy commandments; for therein do I delight" (Ps. 119:35). The psalmist delighted in God's commandments because they moved him into the path of God's blessing for his life. Walking with God in the path of His commandments is always a path of blessing and rejoicing. God's Word guides believers along the path of His will for their lives. They can walk with assurance that God is directing their path according to His will. They need not fear that they will lose their way because God guides His people with loving concern. We should praise God for His faithfulness!

PRAYER

Dear Lord, we praise You for guiding us along the path of Your will. Help us to follow Your leading closely. For Jesus' sake. Amen.

OCTOBER 24

"**W**oe to them that go down to Egypt for help; and stay on horses, and trust in chariots, because they are many; and in horsemen, because they are very strong; but they look not unto the Holy One of Israel, neither seek the Lord!" (Isa. 31:1). It always seems easier to seek worldly help than to seek help from the Lord. But the prophet speaks sternly to those who deliberately seek worldly help and turn away from the Lord. The prophet assures his people that the Lord can defend Jerusalem (vv. 4–5), but they must cast away their idols (vv. 7–8). Every believer should exalt the Lord God to His rightful place as Lord of his life.

PRAYER

Dear Lord, help us to honor You as Lord of all and give us the grace to walk humbly with You and always seek Your help. For Jesus' sake. Amen.

October 25

"**F**rom that time many of his disciples went back, and walked no more with him. Then said Jesus unto the twelve, Will ye also go away?" (John 6:66–67). Peter gave the answer: "Lord, to whom shall we go? thou hast the words of eternal life" (v. 68). The disciples understood that everything depended on the Lord Jesus Christ. If He does not save and sustain His people, we are lost. Our place is to walk with Him on His pathway and trust Him to bring us to His heavenly Father. We may walk with serene confidence. The good shepherd has never lost a sheep. We can know that He leads us to His heavenly Father.

PRAYER

Dear Lord Jesus, help us to follow Your leading and to trust You for every step of the way. Guide our steps homeward. Amen.

OCTOBER 26

David cried, "For I am poor and needy. . . . I am gone like the shadow when it declineth: I am tossed up and down as the locust" (Ps. 109:22–23). David recognized his great need in the sight of God. He was as fleeting as the shadows when the sun sets. He was tossed about like a fragile insect in the wind. But he turned to the Lord in prayer: "Help me, O Lord my God" (v. 26). We too need to turn to the Lord in prayer for our great needs. The Lord God can sustain us, just as He sustained David in His need. David vowed, "I will greatly praise the Lord with my mouth" (v. 30). Let us also praise God for His loving care.

PRAYER

Dear Lord, help us in our great needs. Give us sustaining grace and the sense of Your presence with us. For Jesus' sake. Amen.

OCTOBER 27

"**B**etter is the poor that walketh in his integrity, than he that is perverse in his lips, and is a fool" (Prov. 19:1). The poor man who maintains his integrity and walks with God can be assured of the presence of God with him. The fool who despises God and blurts out whatever he wishes with his mouth is walking a pathway that shall bring him into catastrophic judgment. Men will despise him for his base language, but God will judge him for the sins of his heart and lips. The poor man need not worry; God will provide riches in glory for him, but he should look forward to joyous fellowship and service with the God he honors.

PRAYER

Dear Lord, help us to look beyond our earthly circumstances to that day in which we shall enjoy blessed fellowship with You. For Jesus' sake. Amen.

OCTOBER 28

The Lord said to King Cyrus, "I will go before thee, and make the crooked places straight . . . and I will give thee the treasures of darkness, and hidden riches of secret places, that thou mayest know that I, the Lord, which call thee by thy name, am the God of Israel" (Isa. 45:2–3). The Lord gave special blessing to King Cyrus because he allowed the people of Israel to return to their homeland. God provided him with hidden riches of blessing. The psalmist wrote, "Pray for the peace of Jerusalem: they shall prosper that love thee" (Ps. 122:6). We should pray for the conversion and blessing of Jerusalem at the return of the Lord.

PRAYER

Dear Lord, bring peace and conversion to Your city that Your name may be honored there. For Jesus' sake. Amen.

OCTOBER 29

The man who was born blind testified, "A man that is called Jesus made clay, and anointed mine eyes, and said unto me, Go to the pool of Siloam, and wash: and I went and washed, and I received sight" (John 9:11). It was a simple matter of obedience. The man did exactly what the Lord asked him to do, and Jesus did exactly what He promised. When the blind man learned Who Jesus was, he worshiped Him (v. 38). Every believer should be quick to obey the words of Scripture that the blessing of the Lord might rest upon his path as well. We all need spiritual eyes that are open to the things of the Lord.

PRAYER

Dear Lord, give us an obedient heart and eyes that can see the spiritual blessings that You provide. Amen.

OCTOBER 30

"**I** will run the way of thy commandments, when thou shalt enlarge my heart" (Ps. 119:32). The psalmist understood that he needed internal grace in order to obey the Lord and live his life for the Lord. It is not enough to have a head knowledge of God. The believer needs a personal relationship with God in order to live for Him. The psalmist asked for internal grace from God that he might live his life in a manner pleasing to the Lord. We, too, ought to pray that God would impart to us that grace that would draw us to Him and enable us to please Him by our daily conduct. The believer lives by grace, not by self-effort.

PRAYER

Dear Lord, put within us a heart devotion to You that will enable us to live for You each day. For Jesus' sake. Amen.

OCTOBER 31

"**E**nter not into the path of the wicked, and go not in the way of evil men" (Prov. 4:14). The believer needs discernment to recognize the danger in the path of evil. The wicked rush headlong to destruction, but the believer must turn away into the path of God's will for his life. He needs to turn his back on the evil path and turn his steps toward God. His Word is always a light to lead him to God and His blessing. God's path always leads the believer away from sin, away from the temptations of this world. His Word leads us to the light of His presence and blessing.

PRAYER

Dear Lord, guide our steps to draw ever closer to You. Keep us from the evil path. Guide us by Your Spirit into Your presence. For Jesus' sake. Amen.

NOVEMBER 1

"**F**or ye were as sheep going astray; but are now returned unto the Shepherd and Bishop of your souls" (1 Pet. 2:25). It is easy for people, just like sheep, to go astray. The sheep thinks just of the grass he is eating and not of the danger of the way. Believers need to consider the path they are traveling. Does it lead to dangerous places? Is the Lord calling them to a different direction? It is important for the believer to put himself consciously into the path chosen by the Good Shepherd and to follow Him wherever He leads. He leads to paths of blessing and to a home prepared forever.

PRAYER

Dear Lord, help us to follow You faithfully in the pathway of Your choice. Give us grace and guidance to follow closely. Amen.

November 2

"**B**efore I was afflicted I went astray: but now have I kept thy word" (Ps. 119:67). There are times that afflictions help the believer to draw near to God. No one likes to be afflicted, but if the result is a closer walk with God, the afflictions are beneficial. Believers should walk closer to God without such providential prodding. But we all tend to go our own way without asking the Lord for guidance. We know better, but we tend to blunder forward anyway. Filling the mind with God's Word is a great way of finding direction and guidance on our pathway. Let us continue searching the Scriptures.

PRAYER

Dear Lord, guide us by Your Word. Illumine our path by Your Holy Scriptures. Give us an obedient heart. For Jesus' sake. Amen.

NOVEMBER 3

"**G**o through the gates. . . . Say ye to the daughter of Zion, Behold, thy salvation cometh; behold, his reward is with him, and his work before him" (Isa. 62:10–11). Isaiah prophesied the coming of the great Messiah, Who would redeem His people. The Lord Jesus came to Jerusalem riding upon the colt of an ass to die for the sins of the world (Matt. 21:2–5). Now the Lord offers salvation to all who will trust in Him as Savior. The Lord promised, "All that the Father giveth me shall come to me; and him that cometh to me I will in no wise cast out" (John 6:37). Come to the Savior today.

PRAYER

Dear Lord Jesus, we come to ask for forgiveness, strength, and the grace we need for each day. Help us to trust You for everything. Amen.

NOVEMBER 4

"**T**he children of thy people say, The way of the Lord is not equal: but as for them, their way is not equal. When the righteous turneth from his righteousness . . . he shall even die thereby. . . . But if the wicked turn from his wickedness . . . he shall live thereby" (Ezek. 33:17–18). The Lord is always consistent; it is people who are not consistent. People need to choose the Lord and His Word and stand by their choice. To choose wickedness is to destroy themselves and harm others. We all need to choose wisely for the Lord and turn our backs upon the evil.

PRAYER

Dear Lord, give us grace to turn away from what we know to be evil and to turn to You for grace and help in time of need. For Jesus' sake. Amen.

NOVEMBER 5

The raising of Lazarus was a great testimony to the Jews. "Because that by reason of him many of the Jews went away, and believed on Jesus" (John 12:11). Jesus had stood at Lazarus's tomb and cried, "Lazarus, come forth," and Lazarus came forth alive. In a sense all mankind needs that word of living power. They are dead in sins, and only the Lord Jesus can raise them up and give them life. The Lord Jesus is the resurrection and the life. All believers need His power in their lives and His resurrection promise for the life to come. The Lord Jesus promised, "Because I live, ye shall live also" (John 14:19).

PRAYER

Dear Lord Jesus, help us to live for You and to let our lives shine as a testimony of Your transforming power. Amen.

November 6

"**I**f thou shalt keep all these commandments to do them, which I command thee this day, to love the Lord thy God, and to walk ever in his ways; then shalt thou add three cities more" (Deut. 19:9). Moses was speaking about the cities of refuge. God's blessings are always contingent upon the obedience of His people. If they go astray, the blessings diminish. All God's people must realize that obedience to His Word is the only path of blessing for His people. All other pathways lead away from God. We need to direct our steps to walk with God along the pathway of His will for our lives.

PRAYER

Dear Lord, give us grace to walk with You along the pathway of Your will for our lives. For Jesus' sake. Amen.

NOVEMBER 7

"Whither shall I go from thy spirit? or whither shall I flee from thy presence? If I ascend up into heaven, thou art there: if I make my bed in hell, behold, thou art there" (Ps. 139:7–8). God is present everywhere. To the wicked that is a matter of despair. God is always watching. But to the righteous that is a matter of great comfort and encouragement. God sees every trial and every discouragement. He is always present to help and to guide the believer along his pathway. God never abandons His children. He is present to protect them and to strengthen them in their testimony for Him.

PRAYER

Dear Lord, help us to be conscious of Your presence with us and Your protection and guidance along the path. For Jesus' sake. Amen.

November 8

"**F**olly is joy to him that is destitute of wisdom: but a man of understanding walketh uprightly" (Prov. 15:21). The foolish take pleasure in wicked tricks and sinful pleasures. The wise person thinks ahead and recognizes the harm that such actions can cause and turns away from such deeds. A life of thoughtful consideration for others honors God. A wise person avoids harmful actions, not just for himself but for others as well. The joy he seeks is not harmful to others but is rather beneficial to them. The most important thing about his actions is that God is pleased.

PRAYER

Dear Lord, help us to live in ways that honor You and that bring blessing and encouragement to others. For Jesus' sake. Amen.

NOVEMBER 9

"**T**his is Jerusalem. . . . She hath changed my judgments into wickedness more than the nations, and my statutes more than the countries that are round about her: for they have refused my judgments and my statutes, they have not walked in them" (Ezek. 5:5–6). The prophet sternly charged his people with willful disobedience to God's holy statutes. He charged them with greater sins than the heathen nations around them. God's people must always beware lest they become a bad example for the worldly people who are watching them. We must live for the Lord, and our lives must be testimonies for Him.

PRAYER

Dear Lord, help us to be good examples to all those who know us. Give us the grace to live for You day by day. For Jesus' sake. Amen.

NOVEMBER 10

"**A**nd when he putteth forth his own sheep, he goeth before them, and the sheep follow him: for they know his voice" (John 10:4). The Lord described His own ministry of leading His sheep. Sheep always know the voice of their own shepherd, and they will follow him and no other. The Lord does not drive us before Him; He leads us along the pathway of His will for our lives. In following Him the believer finds the greatest blessings of his life. Our Good Shepherd always leads us to springs of living water and green pastures of sustaining grace. We fear no evil, for He is with us.

PRAYER

Dear Lord, give us grace to follow You wherever You lead. Help us to follow Your leading with trust and obedience. Amen.

NOVEMBER 11

The great messianic king intercedes in behalf of His people: "Let not those that seek thee be confounded for my sake, O God of Israel. Because for thy sake I have borne reproach. . . . For the zeal of thine house hath eaten me up" (Ps. 69:6–7, 9). The Lord Jesus Christ bore that reproach on behalf of His people. We need to stand fast and be prepared to suffer reproach on His behalf. He could say, "In my thirst they gave me vinegar to drink" (Ps. 69:21*b*). Believers need to stand for Him today with true dedication. We are not believers just because things are going well for us.

PRAYER

Dear Lord, thank You for enduring suffering on our behalf. Help us to stand for You regardless of the consequences. Amen.

NOVEMBER 12

"**T**he righteousness of thy testimonies is everlasting: give me understanding, and I shall live" (Ps. 119:144). Believers need wisdom and understanding from God's holy Word. The Bible gives us the right understanding of God and the meaning of life. God invites people to obey His Word and live. The psalmist understood that God's Word can impart wisdom and understanding to the obedient believer. Submission to God's wisdom brings eternal blessings. God's Word is always true and always able to illuminate and transform the believer. We need God's Word that we may live wisely for Him.

PRAYER

Dear Lord, open our eyes to the wisdom of Your Word. Help us to see Your pathway for our lives. For Jesus' sake. Amen.

NOVEMBER 13

Solomon said, "My son, give me thine heart, and let thine eyes observe my ways" (Prov. 23:26). His wisdom was a good example for his children to follow. Every believer must realize that there are people looking to him for an example to follow. If we claim to know the Lord Jesus as Savior, people will look to us as examples to follow. We need to serve the Lord Jesus from the heart so that our lives will be a testimony of devotion to Him. If we act foolishly, we will hurt His cause. If we walk humbly with Him, we can be a blessing and a source of encouragement to others.

PRAYER

Dear Lord, help us to live for You and to be an example to others of a life of devotion to Your cause. Amen.

November 14

"**H**e hath shewed thee, O man, what is good; and what doth the Lord require of thee, but to do justly, and to love mercy, and to walk humbly with thy God?" (Mic. 6:8). The Lord is not unreasonable; He calls people to live rightly and to honor Him. People who are twisted in their thinking violate the laws of God and of man. They should repent of such sins and get right with God and with their fellow man. God calls men to obey His Word and to live lives that honor Him and are a blessing to others. Obedience to God is a path that is open to all. God calls men to turn their backs upon sin and to walk with Him.

PRAYER

Dear Lord, give us grace to forsake lives of self will and sin and to follow Your Word in humble obedience. For Jesus' sake. Amen.

NOVEMBER 15

Jesus said, "Yet a little while is the light with you. Walk while ye have the light, lest darkness come upon you: for he that walketh in darkness knoweth not whither he goeth" (John 12:35). The Lord Jesus is the Light of the World. We need to walk in His light if we are to know God's blessing and favor. Walking with Him means following Him in faith and confidence. He always leads us closer to His Father. As we walk with Him, the light gets brighter each day. He is leading us to the city of light, where His Father dwells and the saints are gathering. It is His eternal home that He is preparing for His people.

PRAYER

Dear Lord Jesus, help us to walk with You day by day and to never forget that You are leading us homeward. Amen.

NOVEMBER 16

King Abijam reigned over Judah, "and he walked in all the sins of his father, which he had done before him" (1 Kings 15:3). The evil influences of a sinful person can be transmitted to the next generation. They have a role model to copy and can easily think that such conduct is "normal." Parents need to think of what they are transmitting to their children. It is not just "things" but traits of character and habit. The memory of parents reading the Scriptures and praying leaves a profound impression on the children. They will remember their prayers for missionaries.

PRAYER

Dear Lord, give us the grace to live lives that are a testimony to all who know us. May they recognize our devotion to You. For Jesus' sake. Amen.

NOVEMBER 17

Asaph prayed concerning his enemies, "Fill their faces with shame, that they may seek thy name, O Lord" (Ps. 83:16). Instead of merely praying for their destruction, Asaph prayed that they might be filled with shame for their evil deeds. It might be that such shame would lead to their repentance and ultimate salvation. We need to learn to pray in like manner for our foes. It may be that God can lead them by whatever pathways are necessary to bring them to a change of heart and life. We must beware of allowing our prayer life to become vindictive. We should always pray that God accomplish His perfect will, especially in the case of our enemies.

PRAYER

Dear Lord, help us to pray, especially for our enemies, that Your perfect will may be accomplished in them. For Jesus' sake. Amen.

November 18

"**W**hoso walketh uprightly shall be saved: but he that is perverse in his ways shall fall at once" (Prov. 28:18). Solomon exhorted his people to walk before the Lord in an upright manner and warned them that walking against the will of the Lord would bring sudden disaster. All believers should remember that warning. We must live our lives as a testimony to the grace and goodness of our God. He will sustain us as we follow the path that His Word marks out before us. All those who walk perversely will find themselves stumbling over the precipice. We need to walk with God.

Prayer

Dear Lord, keep us on the straight and narrow path that leads to Your blessing. For Jesus' sake. Amen.

November 19

"**T**hey shall ask the way to Zion with their faces thitherward, saying, Come, and let us join ourselves to the Lord in a perpetual covenant that shall not be forgotten" (Jer. 50:5). The prophet wrote of a generation of his people that should turn to the Lord in sincerity. They would turn their backs to the world and seek the Lord with all their hearts. We all need that kind of dedication to God. The world is too much with us. We need to seek the Lord with all our hearts and devote ourselves to Him. His love for His people is eternal. We need to turn ourselves away from the world and seek Him with all our hearts.

Prayer

Dear Lord, give us grace to despise the world and to seek You and Your will for our lives above all things. For Jesus' sake. Amen.

November 20

The Lord said to Joshua the high priest, "If thou wilt walk in my ways, and if thou wilt keep my charge, then thou shalt also judge my house, and shalt also keep my courts, and I will give thee places to walk among these that stand by" (Zech. 3:7). If the believer will walk in the ways of the Lord and will keep the charge that the Lord gives him, he will also find that the Lord will give him a place of testimony and service. All such service must be done to please the Lord, not ourselves. We must all ask the Lord to show us what His will is and to give us the grace to do it for Him.

Prayer

Dear Lord, show us the pathway of service You have for us and give us the grace to serve You from the heart. For Jesus' sake. Amen.

NOVEMBER 21

"**A**nd he [Jesus] said to the woman, Thy faith hath saved thee; go in peace" (Luke 7:50). The woman was washing His feet and drying them with the hairs of her head. Simon, the host, sneered because he knew that she was a sinner, but the Lord defended her. He pointed out that the host had not provided water to wash in, nor had he given the Lord a traditional kiss of greeting. The woman, on the other hand, had kissed His feet and washed them with her tears. The Lord pronounced her forgiven, for she loved much and left the Pharisees to wonder whether they loved Him at all.

PRAYER

Dear Lord, help us to serve You out of a heart of love and not to worry about what others may think. For Jesus' sake. Amen.

NOVEMBER 22

It is written of Amon that he did "evil in the sight of the Lord, as his father Manasseh did. And he walked in all the way that his father walked in, and served the idols that his father served, and worshipped them: and he forsook the Lord God of his fathers, and walked not in the way of the Lord." (2 Kings 21:20–22). The example of a father is a powerful force in the life of a child. But all parents are setting an example for their children to follow. If children never see their parents reading the Bible or praying to God, what will they think? Parents who have daily Bible reading and prayer are leaving a lasting impression on their children that will someday bear fruit.

PRAYER

Dear Lord, help us to live in devotion to You that our families may realize how important You are to us. For Jesus' sake. Amen.

NOVEMBER 23

"**M**ake a joyful noise unto the Lord, all ye lands. . . . Enter into his gates with thanksgiving, and into his courts with praise: be thankful unto him, and bless his name" (Ps. 100:1, 4). The apostle Paul exhorted, "Be careful for nothing; but in every thing by prayer and supplication with thanksgiving let your requests be made known unto God. And the peace of God, which passeth all understanding, shall keep your hearts and minds through Christ Jesus" (Phil. 4:6–7). It is well for believers to count their blessings and give thanks to God for His watchful care over His people. How many blessings have we received without ever thanking God for them?

PRAYER

Thank You, Lord for countless blessings that You shower down upon us. Give us a spirit of thanksgiving. For Jesus' sake. Amen.

NOVEMBER 24

"**O** come, let us sing unto the Lord. . . . Let us come before his presence with thanksgiving, and make a joyful noise unto him with psalms" (Ps. 95:1–2). The apostle Paul writes of foods "which God hath created to be received with thanksgiving of them which believe and know the truth" (1 Tim. 4:3). Thanks ought to be the normal response to the blessings of God in our lives. Every believer ought to cultivate a thankful spirit in himself. "Sing unto the Lord with thanksgiving; sing praise upon the harp unto our God" (Ps. 147:7). We need to remember to give thanks for food. "For every creature of God is good, and nothing to be refused, if it be received with thanksgiving" (1 Tim. 4:4).

PRAYER

Thank You, Lord, for all Your bountiful gifts. Help us to keep counting our blessings and thanking You for them. Amen.

NOVEMBER 25

The Lord Jesus said, "Ye have not chosen me, but I have chosen you, and ordained you, that ye should go and bring forth fruit, and that your fruit should remain: that whatsoever ye shall ask of the Father in my name, he may give it you" (John 15:16). The Lord Jesus graciously chose His apostles and gave them a ministry for Him. The souls they reached with the gospel message would be an eternal blessing to them. But He graciously gives all believers opportunities to be a witness for Him. We need to be faithful in telling others about the great Savior we have found. He is still mighty to save.

PRAYER

Dear Lord, help us to remember all Your gracious gifts to us and to live for You in the strength of those gifts. For Jesus' sake. Amen.

NOVEMBER 26

"The way of life is above to the wise, that he may depart from hell beneath" (Prov. 15:24). The believer should always lift up his mind to God above and walk in the wisdom of God's Word. He must keep his mind stayed upon God, for all about him are people who are going down the path of wickedness to hell beneath. "The thoughts of the wicked are an abomination to the Lord" (Prov. 15:26). But "the Lord . . . heareth the prayer of the righteous" (Prov. 15:29). "The fear of the Lord is the instruction of wisdom" (Prov. 15:33). Reverence for God is the wise course of life for His people.

PRAYER

Dear Lord, help us to walk humbly with You, keeping our minds stayed upon You and seeking to please You day by day. For Jesus' sake. Amen.

NOVEMBER 27

Jeremiah warned his people, "Go not forth into the field, nor walk by the way; for the sword of the enemy and fear is on every side" (Jer. 6:25). Jeremiah warned his people against the invading armies that would pillage the countryside and rob all they met. His people needed to repent of their sins and return to the Lord. There are many in our own day that need to turn to the Lord and get right with God. Does it take invading armies to cause people to think of God and His mercy upon the undeserving? We should seek His forgiveness and restoration. Moses prayed, "O satisfy us early with thy mercy" (Ps. 90:14a).

PRAYER

Dear Lord, protect us by Your grace and guard our steps that we may serve You. For Jesus' sake. Amen.

NOVEMBER 28

"**B**ut ye are departed out of the way; ye have caused many to stumble at the law; ye have corrupted the covenant of Levi, saith the Lord of hosts" (Mal. 2:8). In the old dispensation the Jews did not keep the covenant that the Lord made with them. We can all confess that we have not done all the things that we should have done either. At times we have been a poor example for people to follow. But the Lord is gracious. He did not abandon His ancient people, and He will not abandon His people today. The Lord Jesus came into the world to save sinners. He is able to save to the uttermost all those who call upon Him.

PRAYER

Dear Lord, have mercy upon us and direct our steps back to the way of the Lord. Give us grace to follow. For Jesus' sake. Amen.

NOVEMBER 29

Jesus said, "Ye have not chosen me, but I have chosen you, and ordained you, that ye should go and bring forth fruit, and that your fruit should remain: that whatsoever ye shall ask of the Father in my name, he may give it you" (John 15:16). It is a comfort to believers to know that their faith in Christ is not an accident but a choice of the Lord. They should make progress in their faith and bear fruit for Him in their conduct. They should pray to their heavenly Father with serene trust that He hears and will answer according to His perfect will. We need to continue manifesting His love to the brethren (v. 17).

PRAYER

Dear heavenly Father, give us the grace to bear fruit for You in our lives. Help us to live for You in the midst of a wicked world. For Jesus' sake. Amen.

NOVEMBER 30

"**T**he fear of the Lord is a fountain of life, to depart from the snares of death" (Prov. 14:27). Reverence for God is the source for true life. The snares of death await every human being, but God alone is our hope. People cannot live forever in this world; they must prepare for the next. This world is a training ground to prepare for the eternal service of the Lord of the universe. Now we cannot even imagine all that will be involved in serving God forever. We can be sure, however, that He has it all planned out. We need to be quick in seizing the opportunity to serve Him now so that we may be prepared to serve Him forever.

PRAYER

Dear Lord, help us to serve You now so that we may be prepared to serve You in a better way forever. For Jesus' sake. Amen.

DECEMBER 1

Aged Zacharias, father of John the Baptist, prophesied that he would be called "the prophet of the Highest . . . to guide our feet into the way of peace" (Luke 1:76, 79). It was the privilege of John the Baptist to prepare the way for the great Messiah, the Lord Jesus Christ. He is the Prince of Peace. All God's people have a place in God's great plan of redemption. It is a great privilege to point others to the Savior. He came into the world to save sinners. His people should rejoice that they have opportunities to testify for Him. He is the source of all our blessings.

PRAYER

Dear Lord, help us to celebrate Your great salvation in our normal way of living for You. For Jesus' sake. Amen.

DECEMBER 2

"**W**hen thou goest, thy steps shall not be straitened; and when thou runnest, thou shalt not stumble" (Prov. 4:12). The wisdom of God protects believers from going in the wrong pathway or stumbling over obstacles. The proud person forces his way forward no matter what. The person who follows the will of God and walks according to His Word finds a blessed pathway illuminated by the Scriptures themselves. To walk with God is a wonderful privilege. It is the only safe path for the believer, for there are enemies on every hand. God's pathway leads to the home that He has prepared for His children.

PRAYER

Dear Lord, give us grace to follow Your path for our lives. Keep us on the strait and narrow way that leads home. For Jesus' sake. Amen.

DECEMBER 3

"**A** wholesome tongue is a tree of life: but perverseness therein is a breach in the spirit" (Prov. 15:4). In the dry climate of the Holy Land a fruitful tree was a great blessing. In a similar way the tongue of a believer may become a blessing to all around him. His tongue can comfort, encourage, and strengthen those around him. But a person with a perverse tongue can wound the spirit of those around him. Believers should pray that God use their tongues to be a blessing to those around them. Their speech may encourage hearts and draw people to the Lord Jesus Christ.

PRAYER

Dear Lord, help us to use our tongues to strengthen and build up others. Give grace to be a blessing to others. For Jesus' sake. Amen.

December 4

"**I** have spread out my hands all the day unto a rebellious people, which walketh in a way that was not good, after their own thoughts; a people that provoketh me to anger continually to my face" (Isa. 65:2–3). The Lord God pronounces a stern rebuke to His rebellious people. He has invited them to a path of blessing, but they have turned into their own way. All people need to ponder their own pathway in the sight of God. Are they self-willed, provoking God's displeasure? Or are they walking humbly in the path that God has laid out before them? If He is pleased, they are secure. If He is not pleased, they are walking into disaster.

Prayer

Dear Lord, guide our steps into pathways of blessing. Help us to walk with You in humble obedience. For Jesus' sake. Amen.

DECEMBER 5

"**I**f any be a hearer of the word, and not a doer, he is like unto a man beholding his natural face in a [mirror]: for he beholdeth himself, and goeth his way, and straightway forgetteth what manner of man he was" (James 1:23–24). We all need to look into the mirror of God's Word to see ourselves for what we are: sinners in the sight of a holy God. We need the grace of the Lord Jesus Christ to cleanse us from sin and to enable us to live for Him in this wicked world. We must never forget what we were; we need His grace to live for Him and to reach out to others who need His great salvation.

PRAYER

Dear Lord, help us to remember what we were and give us grace to live for You in the midst of this wicked world. For Jesus' sake. Amen.

DECEMBER 6

David sang, "For I have kept the ways of the Lord, and have not wickedly departed from my God. For all his judgments were before me: and as for his statutes, I did not depart from them" (2 Sam. 22:22–23). In contrast to Saul before him, and many of his descendants after him, David sought the Lord with all his heart. He made it a point to search the Scriptures that he had at that time and to seek to please the Lord in his daily life. We also need daily times of study of God's Word and of prayer to our gracious God. We need His blessing on our daily lives and the sense of His presence with us day by day.

PRAYER

Dear Lord, help us to walk with You day by day. Encourage our hearts by Your Word and strengthen us to live for You. For Jesus' sake. Amen.

DECEMBER 7

"**A**s for God, his way is perfect; the word of the Lord is tried: he is a buckler to all them that trust in him. . . . God is my strength and power: and he maketh my way perfect" (2 Sam. 22:31, 33). We also need to walk in the way of the Lord and trust in Him at all times. Our strength is not sufficient; we need God's sustaining grace. We cannot plan our own way because we do not know what the future holds. God's plan is perfect because He knows the future as well as the past. If we walk with Him, He will guide us safely through the trials of life and bring us to Himself right on time.

PRAYER

Dear Lord, give us grace to trust You day by day and to walk Your path for us with faith and confidence in Your guidance. For Jesus' sake. Amen.

DECEMBER 8

The Lord spoke to Solomon in a dream, "If thou wilt walk in my ways, to keep my statutes and my commandments, as thy father David did walk, then I will lengthen thy days" (1 Kings 3:14). The wise king did as the Lord commanded and had a long and prosperous reign. We all need the wisdom to live our lives before God and to serve Him from the heart. To live foolishly is not a benefit to anyone. A wise person thinks about how he can best serve God, how he can be a blessing to his family and those about him. Such meditation leads to a life of blessing and benefit to all.

PRAYER

Dear Lord, give us the wisdom to walk with You and to please You with a life of devotion and service. For Jesus' sake. Amen.

DECEMBER 9

Solomon prayed in behalf of his people, "Then hear thou in heaven, and forgive the sin of thy servants, and of thy people Israel, that thou teach them the good way wherein they should walk" (1 Kings 8:36*a*). We can all be thankful that God hears the prayer of repentant sinners and will restore them to fellowship with Himself. The Lord Jesus invited His people, "Ask, and it shall be given you; seek, and ye shall find; knock, and it shall be opened unto you" (Matt. 7:7). We all need to ask God for the help and grace that we need in our daily life. He is listening. Why not pray?

PRAYER

Dear Lord, have mercy on me and give me the grace I need to obey Your Word and to walk with You. For Jesus' sake. Amen.

DECEMBER 10

"The Lord is my light and my salvation; whom shall I fear? the Lord is the strength of my life; of whom shall I be afraid?" (Ps. 27:1). The protection of the Lord is the believer's greatest security. If He is with us, how can we be afraid? The believer is not an orphan; he is a child of the King. The light of the Lord shines upon him. The Lord is his strength. He can walk the pathway that the Lord opens up before him with the confidence that the Lord will be with him every step of the way. His life is part of God's plan. God will accomplish His purpose through him. Praise God for sustaining grace!

PRAYER

Thank You, Lord, for strengthening me and upholding me in the midst of life's struggles. Give me the grace to walk with You. For Jesus' sake. Amen.

DECEMBER 11

"The labour of the righteous tendeth to life: the fruit of the wicked to sin" (Prov. 10:16). God's people love to share the life that God has graciously given to them in Christ Jesus. They delight in lifting up people to God and His grace. The wicked tend to drag people downward to the sins they themselves are mired in. But God wishes to deliver people from sin. It is the blood of Christ that covers every stain and brings sinners into the presence of God. The righteous love to work toward the salvation of the lost. All men need the grace of God to forsake sin and turn to Christ.

PRAYER

Dear Lord, help us to show people the love of Christ. Give us the grace to bring people to You for salvation. For Jesus' sake. Amen.

DECEMBER 12

"**U**nderstanding is a wellspring of life unto him that hath it: but the instruction of fools is folly" (Prov. 16:22). Solomon commends spiritual understanding to believers. It opens up the refreshing springs of life to those who trust in God. The fool turns away from the wisdom of God to stumble into disaster. The fool sees no harm in sin until it has ruined him. The wise flee from sin and seek the leading of God in pathways of blessing. God's Word directs the believer into safe paths and blessed opportunities of fellowship with God. To learn to walk with God is the meaning of life.

PRAYER

Dear Lord, give us spiritual understanding and grace to walk life's pathway with You. For Jesus' sake. Amen.

DECEMBER 13

"**B**ehold, I will send my messenger, and he shall prepare the way before me: and the Lord, whom ye seek, shall suddenly come to his temple, even the messenger of the covenant, whom ye delight in: behold, he shall come, saith the Lord of hosts" (Mal. 3:1). This is a prophecy of the ministry of John the Baptist, who prepared the way for the coming of the Lord Jesus Christ (Matt. 3). God often uses the faithful testimony of a soulwinner to prepare a person for the message of a preacher. We must all sow the Word of God in faith, knowing that it will not return void (Isa. 55:11).

PRAYER

Dear Lord, help us to be good witnesses for you. Give us the right words that will prepare people for decision for Christ. Amen.

DECEMBER 14

"**B**y faith Abraham, when he was called to go out into a place which he should after receive for an inheritance, obeyed; and he went out, not knowing whither he went" (Heb. 11:8). Abraham lived by his faith in God. He is a good example for us all. We, too, need to obey God's Word and live our lives in submission to His revealed Word. We do not know all the pathway we may be called upon to walk, but we know the God Who has marked out our path and will walk with us on our way. Walking with God is a great privilege. Let us walk with faith and obedience to His will.

PRAYER

Dear Lord, give us grace to walk with You on life's pathway. Guide our steps homeward to You. For Jesus' sake. Amen.

December 15

The prophet recorded concerning Amon king of Judah that "he forsook the Lord God of his fathers, and walked not in the way of the Lord" (2 Kings 21:22). He "served the idols that his father served" (v. 21). He is another example of the sins of the fathers continuing in the children. But his son was Josiah, who began to reign when he was only eight years old (2 Kings 22:1). His mother brought him up to walk in the way of the Lord, and he "turned not aside to the right hand or to the left" (v. 2). This is another example of the influence of godly mothers who train their children in the way of the Lord.

PRAYER

Dear Lord, help us to be an influence for good in the lives of our family and friends. Make us a blessing to others. For Jesus' sake. Amen.

DECEMBER 16

"**L**et the heart of them rejoice that seek the Lord. Seek the Lord, and his strength: seek his face evermore" (Ps. 105:3–4). Seeking the Lord is one of the most joyous things the believer can do. His presence is the source of all our blessings and benefits. We need to seek His strength because ours fails so easily. Seeking His face in glory will be one of our most blessed opportunities for worship and praise. We need to begin now to seek the Lord and to praise His name. We have not thanked Him enough this very day for the abundant blessings we have already received. Let us praise His name for His grace and strength for this day.

PRAYER

Dear Lord, we thank and praise You for your countless blessings this very day. Help us not to forget Your mercies. For Jesus' sake. Amen.

DECEMBER 17

"**H**e that followeth after righteousness and mercy findeth life, righteousness, and honour" (Prov. 21:21). The person who seeks the righteousness and mercy of God will find them. He will also find life and honor as well. But it is eternal life that he finds, for the life of God never ceases. Righteousness and mercy are good virtues to seek and manifest in our daily life. God's people need to live lives that manifest their devotion to Him. Day by day they are building a testimony for Him that others can see. We need to seek His grace and wisdom to be a blessing to others.

PRAYER

Dear Lord, help us to live for You so that our lives may manifest our heart devotion. For Jesus' sake. Amen.

DECEMBER 18

Micah the prophet speaks with scorn of the false prophets of the land, "If a man walking in the spirit and falsehood do lie, saying, I will prophesy unto thee of wine and of strong drink; he shall even be the prophet of this people" (Mic. 2:11). There have always been false prophets who lead people away from God's Word and paths of righteousness. Instead, God's people should follow spiritual leaders who know the Lord and obey His Word. Every believer must keep his own conscience and walk with God. False teachers will lead him into disastrous disobedience to God and His Word.

PRAYER

Dear Lord, guide the steps of Your people. Illumine Your Word to us that we may walk with You according to Your Word. For Jesus' sake. Amen.

DECEMBER 19

"Let us go forth therefore unto him without the camp, bearing his reproach. For here have we no continuing city, but we seek one to come" (Heb. 13:13–14). For a person to be "very religious" is regarded as peculiar by worldly people. This world is not the home of God's people. They have a city above. The Lord Jesus Christ is the center of their interest. He is preparing a place for them, and their hearts are set on seeing Him face to face. Let the world despise and reproach us. His approval is all we need.

PRAYER

Dear Lord, help us to walk our pilgrim pathway with single-minded devotion to You. Give us grace to walk for You. Amen.

DECEMBER 20

"The fear of the Lord tendeth to life: and he that hath it shall abide satisfied; he shall not be visited with evil" (Prov. 19:23). Reverence for God blesses any life. The human heart cannot be satisfied with material things; it yearns for the living God. The presence of God in the life is a protection from the evil influences of a wicked world. The believer needs to be conscious of the presence of the Lord with him. He should be satisfied with the blessing of the Almighty. He should turn his gaze from the wicked world to the Word of God and rejoice in the blessings that he finds in the Holy Scripture.

PRAYER

Dear Lord, help me to be satisfied with the blessings of Your holy Word. Open my eyes to its precious truths. For Jesus' sake. Amen.

December 21

"**F**or I rejoiced greatly, when the brethren came and testified of the truth that is in thee, even as thou walkest in the truth. I have no greater joy than to hear that my children walk in truth" (3 John 3–4). The old apostle John rejoiced to learn that his converts were walking according to the teaching that he had given them. Living out the truth that they learn is important for every believer. Our walk always speaks louder than our words. Consistency in living the Christian life is a powerful testimony to our friends and neighbors. We, too, must live the truth.

PRAYER

Dear Lord, enable me to walk with You according to the truth of Your Word. Give me the grace that I need. For Jesus' sake. Amen.

DECEMBER 22

"**O**rder my steps in thy word: and let not any iniquity have dominion over me" (Ps. 119:133). We, too, need to pray that God will direct our steps through His Word and will break the power of sin in our lives. We need to read His Word with understanding and apply its instruction to our lives. God's Word can break the power of sin in our lives and guide us into paths of service and blessing. We must fill our minds with the teaching of the Word and crowd out the thoughts of evil. Mere willpower cannot deliver us. God's Word is powerful enough to make us what we ought to be.

PRAYER

Dear Lord, fill our minds with the strength of Your Word. Enable us to think of You and to live for You every day. For Jesus' sake. Amen.

DECEMBER 23

The Lord describes His covenant with Levi, "My covenant was with him of life and peace. . . . The law of truth was in his mouth, and iniquity was not found in his lips: he walked with me in peace and equity, and did turn many away from iniquity" (Mal. 2:5–6). Walking with God is a testimony to many who observe. Every believer should remember that others are watching as he travels life's pathway. When he stands firm for the Lord, others take heart and resolve to walk for the Lord themselves. The example of a believer is often a stronger testimony than his words.

PRAYER

Dear Lord, make us a testimony for You. Give us grace to live that others may know that we walk with You. For Jesus' sake. Amen.

DECEMBER 24

Zacharias, father of John the Baptist, gives praise to God at John's birth: "The dayspring from on high hath visited us, to give light to them that sit in darkness and in the shadow of death, to guide our feet into the way of peace" (Luke 1:78–79). John was to prepare the way for the Prince of Peace, the Lord Jesus Christ. All mankind was in the darkness of sin before the Savior came to redeem them by His death on the cross. The Lord Jesus is the Light of the World, Who provides salvation to all who will look to Him for the forgiveness of sins and peace with God. Now believers may walk in the way of peace, knowing that the death of the Savior is the all-sufficient atonement for sin.

PRAYER

Thank You, Lord Jesus, for coming to earth to die for me that I might live with You in heaven. Amen.

December 25

"And being warned of God in a dream that they should not return to Herod, they departed into their own country another way" (Matt. 2:12). God had led the wise men to come to worship at the birth of the great King. After seeing Herod, the star led them to Bethlehem to worship the true King. Then they had to return "another way" in order to avoid being killed by Herod. God leads His obedient people and guides their steps by His grace. We too need to worship the Lord Jesus Christ. He came to earth to die for His people. We need to live for Him and to trust Him to guide our steps the way He guided the wise men. Isaiah prophesied His name, "Immanuel" (Isa. 7:14), "God with us."

Prayer

Thank You, Lord Jesus, for coming to earth to die for us. Help us to live for You in this world and the next. Amen.

December 26

"**F**or the Lamb which is in the midst of the throne shall feed them, and shall lead them unto living fountains of waters: and God shall wipe away all tears from their eyes" (Rev. 7:17). The Lord Jesus will provide eternal blessings for His people. The path that He leads them on leads to Himself. He is their goal. In His presence there will be endless joy and celebration of the goodness and mercy of God. Believers should never forget the purpose of their walk in this life. It is to prepare them for eternity in His presence. Joyous perfection will be their portion.

Prayer

Thank You, Lord, for preparing a place for us in Your presence. Help us to keep our minds stayed on You. For Jesus' sake. Amen.

DECEMBER 27

"**M**oreover thou leddest them in the day by a cloudy pillar; and in the night by a pillar of fire, to give them light in the way wherein they should go" (Neh. 9:12). God did not let His people wander in the wilderness; He gave them clear guidance. We also need the guidance of God in our lives. God has provided that in His precious Word. We need to search the Scriptures daily to find His guidance. His path always leads upward toward His goal for us. We must walk with Him on His path to attain His goal for us. He calls us ever onwards and upwards.

PRAYER

Dear Lord, give grace to follow Your leading and to press onwards to Your goal for our lives. For Jesus' sake. Amen.

December 28

"The Lord our God be with us . . . that he may incline our hearts unto him, to walk in all his ways, and to keep his commandments, and his statutes, and his judgments" (1 Kings 8:57–58). King Solomon's blessing is one that all believers may pray for themselves and their families. We need the Lord with us and His blessing on our lives and our families. The presence of God is the greatest single protection that any person can have. We need to cultivate our daily conversation with Him along life's pathway.

PRAYER

Dear Lord, give us the consciousness of Your presence with us and help us to talk with You as we walk with You. For Jesus' sake. Amen.

DECEMBER 29

"**T**each me to do thy will; for thou art my God: thy spirit is good; lead me into the land of uprightness" (Ps. 143:10). People tend to do their own will. God must teach them to do His will. The Spirit of God gently leads believers to the land of uprightness, where they will seek God's will above their own. We need to be apt pupils, seeking from God's Word the direction we need to walk with God on His pathway. His way leads home; ours may lead to barren lands and hard pathways. God's way is always best, for then we can walk with Him.

PRAYER

Dear Lord, give us the grace to walk humbly with You. Guide us by Your Word to Your home for us. For Jesus' sake. Amen.

DECEMBER 30

"**F**or this God is our God for ever and ever: he will be our guide even unto death" (Ps. 48:14). God guides His people through His Word. He is the eternal God, and His Word is an eternal testimony to His faithfulness. He guides His people not only through this life but through all eternity as well. In His presence is fullness of joy. The saints and angels sing before Him. The promise of the Lord Jesus Christ to His disciples was "because I live, ye shall live also" (John 14:19). Let us live for Him and trust His eternal promises.

PRAYER

Dear Lord, guide our steps through this life and bring us safely into Your presence right on time. For Jesus' sake. Amen.

DECEMBER 31

John saw the victors in heaven, "And they sing the song of Moses the servant of God, and the song of the Lamb, saying, Great and marvellous are thy works, Lord God Almighty; just and true are thy ways, thou King of saints" (Rev. 15:3). There will be singing in heaven. It is not a sad place, but a joyous one. Come and go with me. The Lord Jesus holds out His salvation to all who will believe in Him. His blood can wash you whiter than snow. He can put an eternal song in your heart. Jesus promised those who believed in Him, "I give unto them eternal life; and they shall never perish, neither shall any man pluck them out of my hand" (John 10:28).

PRAYER

Thank You, Lord Jesus, for Your promise; save me and bring me to Your presence right on time. For Your sake. Amen.

Stewart Custer acquired a love for learning as a boy. He writes *The Way of the Lord* as a man who has followed the Lord's path all his life. He and his wife, Carol, recently celebrated their golden wedding anniversary. He is pastor emeritus of Trinity Bible Church in Greenville, South Carolina, where he has served for more than thirty years.

Also by Stewart Custer:

Wonderful Words
#243675

God's Promises New Every Day
#216283